ANSWERS
TO YOUR
QUESTIONS
ABOUT THE
DOCTRINE
AND
COVENANTS

ANSWERS
TO YOUR
QUESTIONS
ABOUT THE
DOCTRINE
AND
COVENANTS

RICHARD O. COWAN

Deseret Book Company
Salt Lake City, Utah

Library of Congress Cataloging-in-Publication Data

Cowan, Richard O., 1934–
    Answers to your questions about the Doctrine and Covenants / by Richard O. Cowan.
        p.   cm.
    Includes bibliographical references and index.
    ISBN 1-57345-201-7 (hardbound)
    1. Doctrine and Covenants—Examinations, questions, etc.
    I. Cowan, Richard O., 1934–   Doctrine & Covenants. II. Title.
BX8628.C68   1996
289.3'2—dc20   96-27337
                                                                   CIP

Printed in the United States of America

10   9   8   7   6   5   4   3   2   1

CONTENTS

PREFACE

It has been my privilege to teach classes on the Doctrine and Covenants at Brigham Young University for more than a third of a century. During that time I have become well acquainted with the questions most frequently asked by the students and also with how they might be answered. Because you may have many of the same questions, this volume has been prepared in the hope that it might help you. Unlike more lengthy works that provide commentary on all Doctrine and Covenants passages, this book attempts only to give concise answers to about three hundred of the questions raised most often.

During the past decade I have collected into a computerized data bank thousands of statements by the General Authorities of the Church relative to specific Doctrine and Covenants passages. This book features some of these statements from the Brethren, which provide clear and authoritative answers to our questions.

This volume also draws material from a variety of published sources, some of which have been long out of print. President Joseph Fielding Smith's *Church History and Modern Revelation,* for example, has been a valuable source for historical and doctrinal insights. Likewise, a dictionary published in 1828 allows us to understand what words meant at the time the revelations in the Doctrine and Covenants were being recorded.

Answers in this volume have been arranged in the numerical order of the sections of the Doctrine and Covenants and are intended to accompany your study of that book of scripture. Similar questions may arise at several different points in the Doctrine and Covenants. In such cases, when you look up the reference to the passage you are studying, you will find either a full answer or a brief response and a cross-reference to the more complete answer. Those cross-references are enclosed in braces and appear in bold type: {See D&C 35:3}.

Quotations have been kept as brief as possible. If you wish to read more extensively from a particular statement, you will find its biblio-graphical data at the end of this book.

The index, which emphasizes doctrinal concepts, will assist you in finding material to answer your questions. Look under similar or related terms until you find what you are seeking.

Of course, you may have questions on the Doctrine and Covenants that are not answered in this volume. But you can follow certain guide-lines to find your own answers.

First, the scriptures themselves set forth the basic principles of the gospel. They are called the standard works because they provide the guidelines by which to judge all concepts and ideas. Hence, a particu-lar passage should be examined in both the broader context of all the scriptures as well as the immediate setting. Knowing the specific cir-cumstances can add meaning to a statement. {See D&C 19:20.}

Second, Church leaders provide valuable insights into how scrip-tural principles apply in today's world. We should recognize the spe-cial stewardship of those whom we sustain as prophets, seers, and revelators. {See D&C 1:38.}

Third, personal revelation is the only way we can ultimately know the truth. {See D&C 5:6–12.} Because scriptures were written under the guidance of the Spirit and because our inspired leaders speak by that same power, we must have the influence of the Spirit ourselves to truly understand their words (see D&C 18:34–36; 50:21–22).

All three of these guidelines should be followed in seeking answers. And sometimes, "I don't know" is the only answer there is for now. The answers in this volume have been prepared with these guide-lines in mind.

THE LORD'S PREFACE

DOCTRINE AND COVENANTS 1

Doctrine and Covenants 1 is placed first in that book of scripture because it was designated by the Lord as his "preface" to the revelations (D&C 1:6). A preface, of course, is where a book's author sets forth his purposes in writing and explains what the reader should expect to gain. Chronologically, however, section 1 was received in November 1831 after section 66 and before section 67.

DOCTRINE AND COVENANTS 1:1-4
What is the basic message of the Doctrine and Covenants and to whom is it directed?

The Lord, the author of the Doctrine and Covenants, sets forth in his "preface" (1:6) that the book's message is "a voice of warning" for "all people." The thrust of his warning is set forth in verse 12: Prepare for the Master's glorious advent, which "is nigh." The need for such a warning is made clear by the description in this revelation of the wicked condition of the world.

DOCTRINE AND COVENANTS 1:16, 36
Why can today's world be called Babylon or Idumea?

The ancient kingdoms of Babylon and Idumea (or Edom) were noted for their hedonistic wickedness. Hence their names are apt labels for today's sinful society, often contrasted with Zion, which is made up of the "pure in heart" (D&C 97:21).

DOCTRINE AND COVENANTS 1:19
Why shouldn't we counsel one another?

The meaning of the phrase "man should not counsel his fellow man" can best be understood in its context. The Lord is reviewing some of the consequences of his having given the revelations contained

1

in the Doctrine and Covenants: the spiritually blessed yet "weak things" (from the world's point of view) will confound the "mighty and strong" (again from the world's viewpoint). Inspired counselors should not rely solely on human wisdom, or, to use Jeremiah's phrase, trust in the arm of flesh (see Jeremiah 17:5). Rather than depending on their own judgment, they can and should "speak in the name of God" (D&C 1:20). Nephi taught this same truth (see 2 Nephi 28:31).

DOCTRINE AND COVENANTS 1:30
In the eyes of the Lord, what is the status of the
restored Church and its members?

The Master affirmed that The Church of Jesus Christ of Latter-day Saints is his "only true and living church." It is unique in having priesthood authority and in teaching the fulness of the gospel. That is why it remains aloof from the ecumenical movement—the increasingly frequent practice of churches to overlook doctrinal or structural differences so they can merge into larger bodies.

"This Church was not formed on man's initiative," taught Elder James E. Talmage; "it was not called into being because of some brilliant leader who stepped forward with a new plan; and therefore we cannot, we have not the power nor the authority, to make any kind of affiliation with any other church; and let me say with equal earnestness, no other denomination, no church, no sect can ever affiliate as such with this, the Church of Jesus Christ of Latter-day Saints. There have been overtures made by some religious bodies to find out the terms under which they probably could come in with us; and the answer has been: Come in as every member of this Church has come in—through . . . the door of baptism, that ye may receive the Holy Ghost by the laying on of hands" (in Conference Report, Apr. 1920, 104).

Still, much good is done by other churches and their members. {See D&C 35:3.} Latter-day Saints on a growing number of occasions have cooperated with these groups to bless the lives of our Father's children in many parts of the world.

The Savior put all this in perspective when he stressed that he was pleased with his Saints "collectively" but not "individually." He explained why, by declaring that he "cannot look upon sin with the least degree of allowance." But he added the welcome assurance that those who repent will be forgiven. (D&C 1:31–32). He chastened his

Saints on a later occasion as well, but once again he did so "collectively but not individually" (D&C 105:2).

DOCTRINE AND COVENANTS 1:35
Is it futile to work for peace?

The Lord has warned that "the day speedily cometh . . . when peace shall be taken from the earth" (D&C 1:35), but we still have the responsibility to promote the cause of peace. {See **D&C 98:16.**} The gospel must be preached worldwide before the Savior's second coming (see Matthew 24:14), and experience has shown that that can best be accomplished during peacetime.

Even though an ultimate goal cannot be realized immediately, we should not overlook ways to do good in the meantime. Elder Glen L. Pace instructed: "We know the prophecies of the future. We know the final outcome. We know the world collectively will not repent and consequently the last days will be filled with much pain and suffering. Therefore, we could throw up our hands and do nothing but pray for the end to come so the millennial reign could begin. To do so would forfeit our right to participate in the grand event we are all awaiting. We must all become players in the winding-up scene, not spectators. We must do all we can to prevent calamities, and then do everything possible to assist and comfort the victims of tragedies that do occur" (*Ensign*, Nov. 1990, 8).

DOCTRINE AND COVENANTS 1:37
What does it mean to "search" the scriptures?

More is involved in searching the scriptures than merely reading or even studying them. We must seek the Spirit so we can more fully understand their meaning (see D&C 18:34–36; 50:21–22).

"As I have read the scriptures," reflected President Marion G. Romney, "I have been challenged by the word ponder. . . . The dictionary says that ponder means 'to weigh mentally, think deeply about, deliberate, meditate.' . . . Pondering is, in my feeling, a form of prayer" (in Conference Report, Apr. 1973, 117).

Our searching of the scriptures is still not complete until we put their precepts into practice in our daily lives (see 1 Nephi 19:23; Matthew 7:24–27).

DOCTRINE AND COVENANTS 1:38
How should we regard the statements of Church leaders?

The scriptures are the standard works, by which the correctness of other statements or concepts can be judged, and the inspired words of our living prophets apply gospel teachings to our present circumstances.

"The most important prophet, so far as we are concerned," affirmed President Ezra Taft Benson, "is the one who is living in our day and age. This is the prophet who has today's instructions from God to us today. God's revelation to Adam did not instruct Noah how to build the ark. Every generation has need of the ancient scripture plus the current scripture from the living prophet. Therefore, the most crucial reading and pondering which you should do is of the latest inspired words from the Lord's mouthpiece. That is why it is essential that you have access to and carefully read his words in current Church publications" (in Korea Area Conference Report, 1975, 52).

President J. Reuben Clark Jr. explained which of our Church leaders may add to the standard works: "Only the President of the Church, the Presiding High Priest, is sustained as Prophet, Seer, and Revelator for the Church, and he alone has the right to receive revelations for the Church, either new or amendatory, or to give authoritative interpretations of scriptures that shall be binding on the Church, or change in any way the existing doctrines of the Church." No other person may do any of these things "unless he has special authorization from the President of the Church." President Clark explained that the counselors in the First Presidency and the members of the Twelve are also "sustained as prophets, seers, and revelators, which gives them a special spiritual endowment in connection with their teaching" (*Church News,* 31 July 1954, 9–10).

President Harold B. Lee emphasized that in general conferences we hear "more inspired declarations on most every subject and problem about which [we] have been worrying. If you want to know what the Lord would have the Saints know and to have his guidance and direction for the next six months, get a copy of the proceedings of this conference, and you will have the latest word of the Lord as far as the Saints are concerned" (in Conference Report, Oct. 1973, 168).

JOSEPH SMITH BEGINS HIS MINISTRY

DOCTRINE AND COVENANTS 2 THROUGH 12

The latter-day restoration of the gospel began in the early spring of 1820. Although the First Vision is not recorded in the Doctrine and Covenants, it provides an essential foundation to the revelations that are included in that book. Among the other things Joseph Smith learned in that vision are that God lives and answers prayers, that the Father and the Son are distinct glorious beings, that the fulness of the gospel needed to be restored, and that Satan's opposing power is real. An account of this significant experience is included in the Pearl of Great Price in Joseph Smith–History 1:15–20.

The revelations recorded in Doctrine and Covenants 2 through 12 begin with Moroni's appearance in 1823 and continue with other revelations received by 1829. Several are related to the coming forth of the Book of Mormon. In these revelations we are introduced to such key figures of the Restoration as Martin Harris, Oliver Cowdery, the Prophet's father, and the Prophet's brother Hyrum.

DOCTRINE AND COVENANTS 2
Why is the wording of Malachi's prophecy not the same here as it is in the Bible?

As Moroni told Joseph Smith about the Book of Mormon record, he cited several prophecies of latter-day events to emphasize that it was important for the gospel to be preached in preparation for the Lord's second coming (see Joseph Smith–History 1:36–41). Because he did not quote Malachi 4:5–6 exactly, some have supposed that Moroni was correcting errors in biblical translation; however, when the Savior visited ancient America, he quoted Malachi's prophecy about Elijah just as it reads in the Bible (see 3 Nephi 25:5–6). Moroni's paraphrase of Malachi's words emphasized certain concepts: Elijah would restore priesthood authority, promises had been made to the fathers, and Elijah's coming was vital.

DOCTRINE AND COVENANTS 2:1
What authority did Elijah restore?

Elijah appeared personally in 1836 and restored the sealing keys of the priesthood by which all earthly ordinances, not just those in the temple, are recognized in heaven. {See **D&C 110:13–16.**}

DOCTRINE AND COVENANTS 2:1
What is "the great and dreadful day of the Lord"?

President Joseph Fielding Smith was convinced that "the great and dreadful day of the Lord" will be at the beginning of the Millennium: "This great and dreadful day can be no other time than the coming of Jesus Christ to establish his kingdom in power on the earth, and to cleanse it from all iniquity. It will not be a day of dread and fear to the righteous, but it will be a day of fear and terror to the ungodly" (*Doctrines of Salvation,* 1:173).

DOCTRINE AND COVENANTS 2:2
What "promises" were made to the "fathers"?

President Joseph Fielding Smith taught concerning the promises made to the fathers:

"This expression has reference to certain promises made to those who died without a knowledge of the gospel, and without the opportunity of receiving the sealing ordinances of the Priesthood in matters pertaining to their exaltation. According to these promises, the children in the latter days are to perform all such ordinances in behalf of the dead" (*Improvement Era,* July 1922, 829; see also Smith, *Doctrines of Salvation,* 2:127–28).

"Why is it that sometimes only one of a city or household receives the gospel?" asked Elder Melvin J. Ballard. "It was made known to me that it is because of the righteous dead who had received the gospel in the spirit world exercising themselves, and in answer to their prayers elders of the Church were sent to the homes of their posterity that the gospel might be taught to them, and through their righteousness they might be privileged to have a descendant in the flesh do the work for their dead kindred. I want to say to you that it is with greater intensity that the hearts of the fathers and mothers in the spirit world are turned to their children than that our hearts are turned to them" (in Hinckley, *Sermons and Missionary Services of Melvin Joseph Ballard,* 249).

Elder Ballard further testified: "The spirit and influence of your dead will guide those who are interested in finding those records. If there is anywhere on the earth anything concerning them, you will find it" (in Hinckley, *Sermons and Missionary Services of Melvin Joseph Ballard,* 230).

President Harold B. Lee suggested another way of looking at Malachi's prophecy as it is recorded in Doctrine and Covenants 2: "Today that scripture undoubtedly has a more significant meaning. Unless the hearts of the children are turned to their parents and the hearts of the parents are turned to their children in this day, in mortality, the earth will be utterly wasted at His coming. There was never a time when so much was needed as today in the homes of the Latter-day Saints and the world generally. Most of the ills that afflict youth today are because of the breakdown in the homes. The hearts of the fathers must be turned to their children, and the children to their fathers, if this world is going to be saved and the people prepared for the coming of the Lord" (*Teachings of Harold B. Lee,* 283).

As we become aware of these promises, our thoughts naturally turn to our own ancestors, whom it is our privilege and responsibility to help. The resulting interest in family history has appropriately been called "having the spirit of Elijah."

DOCTRINE AND COVENANTS 3:2
How can God's paths be "straight" and at the same time "round"?

Just as a wedding ring symbolizes eternity because it has no beginning nor end, so God's purposes are eternal in scope, and he consistently moves "straight" toward achieving them.

DOCTRINE AND COVENANTS 3:17
Weren't all the Nephites killed at Cumorah?

Although the Nephites as a nation were destroyed by the Lamanites in this final great battle, not all of the descendants of Nephi were killed. There had been an extensive mixing of the posterities of Nephi and Laman before Christ's appearance after his resurrection (see, for example, Alma 2; 23–24; 46–47; Helaman 4–6). There was an even more thorough mixing during the two centuries of peace after the

Savior's visit when there were no Nephites, Lamanites, "nor any manner of -ites" (4 Nephi 1:15–17). Hence both groups at Cumorah included descendants of both Nephi and Laman.

DOCTRINE AND COVENANTS 4:1
What is the "marvelous work" prophesied
to come forth in the latter days?

The ancient prophet Isaiah looked forward to the latter days when God would accomplish "a marvellous work and a wonder" (Isaiah 29:14). President Joseph Fielding Smith explained: "This marvelous work is the restoration of the Church and the Gospel with all the power and authority[,] keys and blessings which pertain to this great work for the salvation of the children of men" (*Church History and Modern Revelation,* 1:35).

Joseph Smith was only twenty-three years old when he received the revelation recorded in Doctrine and Covenants 4. "Unknown, untaught, with no reputation, he should have been forgotten in the small hamlet, almost nameless, in the backwoods of a great state," declared Elder John A. Widtsoe, "but he dared to say that the work that he was doing, under God's instruction, was to become a marvel and a wonder in the world. . . . The truths set loose by the Prophet Joseph Smith have touched every man of faith throughout the whole civilized world, and measurably changed their beliefs for good" (in Conference Report, Apr. 1946, 21–22).

DOCTRINE AND COVENANTS 4:2
How can we serve with all our "heart, might, mind and strength"?

Elder Sterling W. Sill explained that we must "coordinate all of our powers into one cooperative effort. This involves a joint action of heart, mind, might, and strength.

"To serve Him with all our hearts means that our love and devotion should be genuine and complete. To serve Him with all our might is to employ to the utmost our determination, commitment, and willpower. It does not mean to walk the irregular pathway of vacillation and procrastination. To serve Him with all our mind requires a strong, positive mental attitude. It means continual study, thoughtfulness, meditation, and firm, positive decisions on each of the questions involved. To serve Him with all of our strength requires vigorous, persistent, continuous physical activity.

"By this process of consolidation and joint action one may concentrate all of the elements of personal effectiveness into one united, fiery, and powerful effort" (*New Era*, Sept. 1985, 4–5).

"We cannot just be in the Church in a casual or disinterested way," emphasized Elder Mark E. Petersen. "Indifference has no place in the heart or mind of a Latter-day Saint. If we are going to be Latter-day Saints, we must do something about it" (*Commitment to Temple Marriage*, 3).

DOCTRINE AND COVENANTS 4:3
Don't we need authority before we can serve God?

Doctrine and Covenants 4:3 does not specifically mention the need for authority, but this verse must be understood in the context of many other scriptures that do specify that priesthood is necessary when one performs ordinances or acts in any official capacity (see, for example, Hebrews 5:4; John 15:16; D&C 42:11). Not long after this scripture was given, the Lord cautioned: "You need not suppose that you are called to preach until you are called" (D&C 11:15).

Still, there is much that we can be and should be doing in unofficial ways without waiting to be commanded (see D&C 58:26–28). The Master taught a similar principle when he directed his disciples to go the second mile (see Matthew 5:41). We all have experienced the exhilarating satisfaction that comes from doing good on our own initiative.

DOCTRINE AND COVENANTS 4:4
What is meant by the "field" being "white already to harvest"?

The Lord has compared his work on earth to harvesting crops in a field or a vineyard (see Matthew 9:37–38; John 4:35–36). The heads of grain in a field take on a white color when they are ready to be harvested. The field is not "all ready to harvest" but is "already to harvest"—that is, the harvest is not just about to begin but is now in progress. Hence our need to get involved is urgent. {See D&C 31:4.}

DOCTRINE AND COVENANTS 4:4
How does sharing the gospel bring salvation to our own souls?

The muscles of our physical bodies weaken and atrophy if we go a prolonged time without using them. Vigorous exercise, on the other

9

hand, strengthens our body. Similarly, we exercise and strengthen our testimony as we share it with others. We are more likely to keep the commandments if we are seeking to set a good example for the person we are teaching. Furthermore, being accompanied by those with whom we have shared the gospel will increase our own joy as we enter God's kingdom (see D&C 18:15–16).

"By reclaiming an erring brother, we save both him and ourselves," testified Elder Bruce R. McConkie. "Our sins are hidden (remitted) because we ministered for the salvation and blessing of another" (*Doctrinal New Testament Commentary*, 3:279).

DOCTRINE AND COVENANTS 4:5–7
What do these attributes mean?

President David O. McKay noted that the Lord listed "essential qualifications of those who were to participate in the bringing about of this marvelous work. These qualifications were not the possession of wealth, not social distinction, not political preferment, not military achievement, not nobility of birth; but a desire to serve God with all your 'heart, might, mind and strength'—spiritual qualities that contribute to nobility of soul" (in Conference Report, Oct. 1966, 86).

"Charity is the pure love of Christ" (Moroni 7:47). Elder Bruce R. McConkie explained: "It is love so centered in righteousness that the possessor has no aim or desire except for the eternal welfare of his own soul and for the souls of those around him" (*Mormon Doctrine*, 121).

Elder Hartman Rector Jr. affirmed: "The eye single to the glory of God is crucial. This means . . . instead of forever doing what we want to do, we must do what the Lord wants done" (*Improvement Era*, Dec. 1969, 81).

President Ezra Taft Benson declared that one who is patient "will be tolerant of the mistakes and failings of his loved ones. Because he loves them, he will not find fault nor criticize nor blame" (in Conference Report, Oct. 1983, 62).

Elder McConkie wrote: "Kindness embraces an interest in another's welfare and a disposition to be helpful" (*Mormon Doctrine*, 413–14).

President Benson also taught that a person who is temperate "is restrained in his emotions and verbal expressions. He does things in moderation and is not given to overindulgence. In a word, he has self-control. He is the master of his emotions, not the other way around" (in Conference Report, Oct. 1983, 61).

It is obvious how these attributes can help us in our Church assignments, in relationships at home, and in all the other aspects of our lives. Think of the opposite of each characteristic—fear rather than faith, lack of focus rather than an eye single to God's glory, and so forth—and consider how these negative traits thwart our effectiveness.

DOCTRINE AND COVENANTS 5:6–12
How can we know the truth?

Over the centuries philosophers have debated how we can learn truth. Some have taught that our physical senses are the only means of knowing what actually exists—but the senses can be deceived. Others have insisted that reason is the only way to be sure our thinking is logically consistent—but our ideas might have no connection with reality. Still other philosophers have suggested that both the senses and reason must be employed together. Even this combined approach, however, falls short of giving us a sure knowledge of spiritual truths.

The Lord's revelations shed light on this age-old question. When Martin Harris asked to see the plates containing the Book of Mormon, the Lord replied that the unbelieving world would not be convinced even if Joseph Smith "should show them all these things" (D&C 5:7). Human sight and reason were not enough without the confirming witness of the Spirit. The Lord then specified that we must receive his word through the Prophet (see D&C 5:10). We can also rely on the testimony of other witnesses who have learned the truth by revelation from heaven (see D&C 5:11–12).

We must personally pay a price to know the truth. The Lord told Martin Harris that he needed to humble himself and repent of his sins to know the truth (see D&C 5:24–28). Oliver Cowdery learned that he needed to have his priorities in order (see D&C 6:7) and that he truly had to desire this knowledge (see D&C 6:8, 20, 22, 25). He also needed to ask in faith (see D&C 8:1; compare Moroni 10:4), and mental exertion must also be involved (see D&C 8:2; 9:7–9).

DOCTRINE AND COVENANTS 6:1–6
Why is exactly the same wording repeated at the beginning of several different revelations?

The opening verses of Doctrine and Covenants 6, 11, 12, and 14 are identical, repeating many of the points revealed in section 4. The general ideas contained in these verses are a fitting preface to the specific assignments given to the brethren addressed in those revelations.

DOCTRINE AND COVENANTS 6:7
Should we shun worldly wealth?

As the Lord counseled Oliver Cowdery about proper priorities, he admonished him to put spiritual goals ahead of temporal concerns (compare Matthew 6:33). The use of riches and our attitude toward them determine whether they are a positive or a negative force in our lives. {See D&C 56:16–18.} Jacob made a similar point in the Book of Mormon when he declared that after obtaining spiritual treasures we can seek temporal wealth because we would do so in the right way and for the right reasons (see Jacob 2:17–19).

DOCTRINE AND COVENANTS 6:7
Shouldn't we leave the mysteries alone?

A mystery is something we cannot know through human resources alone but can learn only by divine revelation. {See D&C 5:6–12.} Where such "mysteries" as the exact date of the Second Coming or the precise meaning of symbols in the Revelation of John have not been revealed, we should follow Alma's example and leave them alone (see Alma 37:11). The "mysteries" that have been unfolded to the righteous include such gospel truths as the forgiveness of sins through Christ's atonement, life after death, and many others. {See D&C 84:19–22.} These can be understood only through obedience to God's law (see D&C 63:23).

"The Lord has promised to reveal his mysteries to those who serve him in faithfulness," explained President Joseph Fielding Smith. "There are no mysteries pertaining to the Gospel, only as we, in our weakness, fail to comprehend Gospel truth. The Gospel is very simple, so that even children at the age of accountability may understand it. Without question, there are principles which in this life we cannot understand, but when the fulness comes we will see that all is plain and reasonable and within our comprehension. The 'simple' principles of the Gospel, such as baptism [and] the atonement, are mysteries to those who do not have the guidance of the Spirit of the Lord" (*Church History and Modern Revelation*, 1:43).

DOCTRINE AND COVENANTS 6:9
How can we "say nothing but repentance"?

President Joseph Fielding Smith pointed out: "When the Lord calls upon his servants to cry nothing but repentance, he does not mean that they may not cry baptism, and call upon the people to obey the commandments of the Lord, but he wishes that all that they say and do be in the spirit of bringing the people to repentance. Any missionary who fails to do this in his ministry is derelict in his duty" (*Church History and Modern Revelation,* 1:57). Even though we may teach a variety of topics, we should always do so in such a way that our listeners will want to repent and improve their lives.

DOCTRINE AND COVENANTS 6:32
What is the significance of adding the phrase "as touching one thing" to the Lord's words in Matthew 18:20?

The addition of this phrase emphasizes that we must be united in a righteous purpose. Even if there are only two or three of us, with the Lord's help we cannot fail (see Genesis 18:14; Luke 1:37).

DOCTRINE AND COVENANTS 7:2
What is the nature of "translated beings," and what is their purpose?

John the apostle became a "translated being." Joseph Smith observed that many have supposed that translated beings "were taken immediately into the presence of God and into an eternal fullness, but [that] is a mistaken idea. Their place of habitation is that of the terrestrial order." The Prophet explained that translated beings obtain "deliverance from the tortures and sufferings of the body" so that their service and existence may be prolonged until they can be resurrected and "enter into so great a rest and glory" (*Teachings of the Prophet Joseph Smith,* 170, 171).

The three Nephite disciples, for example, underwent one change—being quickened from their telestial state to a higher terrestrial level. A greater change would accompany Christ's second coming, equivalent to death and resurrection, resulting in their being moved from mortality to immortality "in the twinkling of an eye" (3 Nephi 28:8; see also vv. 7, 9, 36–40).

The three Nephite disciples were also promised that they would never "taste of death" nor "endure the pains of death." This promise did not mean they would never die. Compare this promise with a similar statement in Doctrine and Covenants 42:46 that the righteous who "die in me shall not taste of death, for it shall be sweet unto them."

Joseph Smith taught that "translated bodies are designed for future missions" (*Teachings of the Prophet Joseph Smith*, 191). For example, Moses and Elias (or Elijah) bestowed the keys of the priesthood on Peter, James, and John on the Mount of Transfiguration before Christ inaugurated the resurrection (see *Teachings of the Prophet Joseph Smith*, 158). Because this bestowal is done by the laying on of physical hands, Moses and Elijah had to be blessed in such a way that they might retain their mortal bodies much longer than the normal life span. Similarly, John the Revelator (see John 21:20–23) and the three Nephite disciples (see 3 Nephi 28) were translated so that they could remain on earth and labor to prepare the world for Christ's second coming.

DOCTRINE AND COVENANTS 9:5–11
Did Oliver Cowdery realize his desire to translate?

While emphasizing that Oliver had to do more than simply ask, we often forget that he "began to translate" but "did not continue" (D&C 9:5). As had happened with Peter when he stepped out of the boat to walk on the water, Oliver "feared," and so he lost his gift (D&C 9:11; see Matthew 14:11, 26–31). Exactly how much Oliver Cowdery translated is not known.

DOCTRINE AND COVENANTS 9:7–9
Must a burning witness always accompany answers to prayer?

A "burning in the bosom" may accompany answers to prayer, but it is by no means required. Perhaps even more often we may feel a calm assurance, as Oliver Cowdery did (see D&C 6:22–23).

President Marion G. Romney explained, "When confronted with a problem I prayerfully weigh in my mind alternative solutions and come to a conclusion as to which of them is best. Then in prayer I submit to the Lord my problem, tell him I desire to make the right choice, what is, in my judgment, the right course. Then I ask him if I have made the right decision to give me the burning in my bosom that He promised Oliver Cowdery. When enlightenment and peace come into my mind, I know the Lord is saying yes. If I have a 'stupor of thought,'

I know he is saying no, and I try again, following the same procedure" (*New Era,* Oct. 1975, 35).

Elder Boyd K. Packer counseled: "Put difficult questions in the back of your minds and go about your lives. Ponder and pray quietly and persistently about them.

"The answer may not come as a lightning bolt. It may come as a little inspiration here and a little there, 'line upon line, precept upon precept' (D&C 98:12).

"Some answers will come from reading the scriptures, some from hearing speakers. And, occasionally, when it is important, some will come by very direct and powerful inspiration. The promptings will be clear and unmistakable" (in Conference Report, Oct. 1979, 30).

DOCTRINE AND COVENANTS 10:6–7
In what way did Martin Harris seek to destroy Joseph Smith's work?

We usually think of Martin Harris as one of the Prophet's supporters. He had helped with the initial phases of translation and later provided substantial financial help for publishing the Book of Mormon. Nevertheless, his persistently asking to show the Book of Mormon manuscript to others even after the Lord had denied permission resulted in its being lost and in Joseph Smith's temporarily losing his gift to translate (compare Doctrine and Covenants 88:64–65). Similarly, we may not consciously choose to do wrong, but we sometimes persist in doing things that are unwise and whose ultimate negative consequences we do not even remotely comprehend.

DOCTRINE AND COVENANTS 10:8–46
How did the Lord thwart Satan's plan to destroy the Book of Mormon?

Joseph Smith learned by revelation that his enemies planned to alter some portions of the lost manuscript to discredit his power to translate (see D&C 10:15–18). The ancient prophet Nephi testified that the Lord, knowing all things, had hundreds of years earlier provided the means to thwart this plot. Specifically, "for a wise purpose" known only to God, Nephi was directed to prepare two parallel records: the large plates, containing a secular history of the kings and their wars, and the small plates, containing an account of the prophets' ministry (see 1 Nephi 9:2–6). Both histories began with the colony's departure from Jerusalem in 600 B.C. and continued until about 150 B.C., when the small plates were filled. This same period was covered by the book of Lehi on the large plates. After this date, beginning with the book of Mosiah, the large plates were used to record an integrated secular and spiritual history. Later, Mormon abridged the history on the large plates of Nephi.

Joseph Smith began his translation with Mormon's abridgment of the book of Lehi; this was the 116 pages Martin Harris lost. Rather than having Joseph retranslate this same material (which had now been altered by those who had stolen the manuscript), the Lord directed him to substitute the parallel and superior spiritual account from the small plates (1 Nephi–Omni 1).

The revelation in Doctrine and Covenants 10 explained that the lost material was "engraved on the [large] plates of Nephi," but "a more particular account" of spiritual things was "upon the [small] plates of Nephi." Therefore "translate the engravings which are on the [small] plates of Nephi until you come to the reign of king Benjamin [introduced in the book of Omni] . . . and thus I will confound those who have altered my words. . . . Behold, there are many things engraved on the [small] plates of Nephi which do throw greater views upon my gospel." The "remainder" of the large plates also contains "all those parts of my gospel" (D&C 10:41–46). Hence none of the spiritual history recorded in the Book of Mormon was lost.

DOCTRINE AND COVENANTS 10:19–22
What are Satan's objectives, and how does he go about achieving them?

After his rebellion against God's plan in the premortal councils (see D&C 29:36–38 and Moses 4:1–4), Satan and his followers were cast out of heaven and lost the privilege of obtaining physical bodies. Thus they could never become living souls composed of a spirit and a physical body (see D&C 88:15) capable of receiving "a fullness of joy" (D&C 93:33). Jealous that we have what he can never obtain, Satan wants to make us miserable, even as he is (see 2 Nephi 2:27). He seeks to destroy our souls as well as God's work on earth (see D&C 10:22–23).

Satan still uses the tactics described in Doctrine and Covenants 10:20, 24, and 25 and in 2 Nephi 28:20–22. Not only does he stir up open opposition but he more subtly tries to make us believe there are no absolute standards of right or wrong. By creating a false sense of security, he lulls us into spiritual apathy. Knowing what these tactics are can alert us to avoid them.

DOCTRINE AND COVENANTS 11:30
Because we all are spirit sons and daughters of our Heavenly Father, in what other sense may we become his children?

Even as our earthly parents have given us physical birth, so our heavenly parents earlier gave us spirit birth. King Benjamin taught that as we repent, become truly converted, and receive saving gospel ordinances, we become "the children of Christ" (Mosiah 5:7; see also Moses 8:13). In a sense he becomes the father of our spiritual rebirth through the marvelous power of his atonement. As his adopted children we can properly inherit his kingdom.

THE PRIESTHOOD AND THE CHURCH RESTORED

DOCTRINE AND COVENANTS 13 THROUGH 22

During the eventful year from the spring of 1829 to the spring of 1830, the priesthood was restored, the Book of Mormon was published, and the Church was organized. In addition, the revelations recorded in sections 13 through 22 were accepted as "the church articles and covenants" (D&C 33:14). {See D&C 33:14.}

DOCTRINE AND COVENANTS 13
What is meant by "the ministering of angels"?

Those holding the Aaronic Priesthood may receive the assistance of angels. For example, President Wilford Woodruff testified, "I had the administration of angels while holding the office of a priest. I had visions and revelations. I traveled thousands of miles. I baptized men, though I could not confirm them because I had not the authority to do it" (*Discourses of Wilford Woodruff*, 298). Nevertheless, President Woodruff cautioned, "The Lord never did nor never will send an angel to anybody merely to gratify the desire of the individual to see an angel. If the Lord sends an angel to anyone, He sends him to perform a work that cannot be performed [except] by the administration of an angel" (*Deseret Weekly News*, 55:21; in Otten and Caldwell, *Sacred Truths*, 1:63).

If we associate temporal affairs with the lesser priesthood and spiritual matters with the higher, we may wonder why such a remarkable manifestation as the "ministering of angels" is linked with the Aaronic rather than the Melchizedek Priesthood. As great as this blessing is, the higher priesthood makes possible an even greater one (see D&C 84:19–22; 107:19–20).

DOCTRINE AND COVENANTS 13
Who are the "sons of Levi," and what is their offering?

The answer to this question may be understood on at least two levels. On the literal level, Joseph Smith explained that the Savior's atonement did not completely end blood offerings. "These sacrifices as well as every ordinance, belonging to the priesthood, will, when the Temple of the Lord shall be built, and the sons of Levi be purified, be fully restored and attended to" (*Teachings of the Prophet Joseph Smith,* 173).

President Joseph Fielding Smith explained why that must take place. "We are living in the dispensation of the fulness of times into which all things are to be gathered, and all things are to be restored since the beginning. . . . It will be necessary, therefore, for the sons of Levi, who offered the blood sacrifices anciently in Israel, to offer such a sacrifice again to round out and complete this ordinance in this dispensation" (*Doctrines of Salvation*, 3:94).

On a more figurative level, the Lord promised that faithful bearers of the Melchizedek and Aaronic Priesthood who magnify their callings "become the sons of Moses and of Aaron" respectively (D&C 84:33–34). Because Moses and Aaron were members of the tribe of Levi, faithful latter-day priesthood bearers become the "sons of Levi," and their "offering" is the faithful service they render (see, for example, D&C 128:24).

DOCTRINE AND COVENANTS 13
Will the Aaronic Priesthood be taken from the earth again?

John the Baptist declared that the lesser priesthood must be on earth "until the sons of Levi do offer again an offering unto the Lord in righteousness" (D&C 13:1). The word *until* has several meanings. It may mean that something will cease to exist when a certain point is reached, but it does not necessarily have to mean that. The Lord affirmed that the Aaronic Priesthood will continue forever along with the higher Melchizedek Priesthood (see D&C 84:18). Oliver Cowdery recalled John's words slightly differently: "Upon you my fellow-servants, in the name of Messiah, I confer this Priesthood and this authority, which shall remain upon earth, that the sons of Levi may yet offer an offering unto the Lord in righteousness" (Pearl of Great Price, note following Joseph Smith–History 1:75). There is no suggestion that the priesthood will ever be taken away.

DOCTRINE AND COVENANTS 13

After John the Baptist conferred the Aaronic Priesthood upon Joseph Smith and Oliver Cowdery, he instructed them to baptize and ordain each other (see Joseph Smith–History 1:68–71). Why did he have them do that rather than perform these ordinances himself?

Baptism, confirmation, and ordination to the priesthood are earthly ordinances that must be performed by mortals living on the earth. Performing these ordinances under John's direction gave Joseph and Oliver valuable training and experience.

DOCTRINE AND COVENANTS 18:9

Had the Melchizedek Priesthood already been restored when this revelation was received?

The Lord reminded Oliver Cowdery and David Whitmer that they had the same calling as Paul the apostle. Although the record of Peter, James, and John restoring the Melchizedek Priesthood has been lost, many students of the Doctrine and Covenants believe this verse indicates that Oliver Cowdery and David Whitmer did have the higher priesthood by the time this revelation was received in June 1829. The Melchizedek Priesthood was restored on the banks of the Susquehanna River in the "wilderness" between Harmony, Pennsylvania, and Colesville, New York (D&C 128:20). Joseph Smith and Oliver Cowdery left the Susquehanna River country and moved about one hundred miles to Fayette, New York, about 1 June 1829, "and there resided until the translation [of the Book of Mormon] was finished" (*History of the Church*, 1:48–49). Hence, the restoration of the higher priesthood had likely occurred before this move (see Porter, "Restoration of the Priesthood").

DOCTRINE AND COVENANTS 18:20

What is "the church of the devil"?

Nephi was told that ultimately there are only two churches: "the one is the church of the Lamb of God, and the other is the church of the devil" (1 Nephi 14:10). In one of the first revelations given through Joseph Smith, the Lord declared that His church consists only of those who repent and come unto Him (see D&C 10:67–68). Thus anything or anyone that diverts us from the Lord or from keeping his commandments is of the church of the devil. {See D&C 1:30.}

"In other words," reasoned Elder Bruce R. McConkie, "the church of the devil is the world; it is all the carnality and evil to which fallen man is heir; it is every unholy and wicked practice; it is every false religion, every supposed system of salvation which does not actually save and exalt man in the highest heaven of the celestial world" (*Doctrinal New Testament Commentary*, 3:551).

President Joseph Fielding Smith concluded, "When we are commanded to 'contend against no church save it be the church of the devil,' we must understand that this is instruction to us to contend against all evil, that which is opposed to righteousness and truth. . . . All who go forth to teach should do so in wisdom and not contend with the churches or engage in profitless debates, but teach in the spirit of kindness and try to persuade people to receive the truth" (*Church History and Modern Revelation*, 1:83).

The Master has directed us not to argue over tenets but rather to proclaim his gospel, which counters the forces of evil and brings people to him (see D&C 19:29–31).

DOCTRINE AND COVENANTS 18:34–36
Why is it so important to study the scriptures by the power of the Spirit?

The scriptures were written by prophets "as they were moved by the Holy Ghost" (2 Peter 1:21; compare D&C 68:4) and hence must be understood by that same Spirit (see 1 Corinthians 2:11–14). The Doctrine and Covenants similarly teaches that those who speak (or write) and those who listen (or read) by the Spirit truly "understand one another, and both are edified and rejoice together" (D&C 50:21–22). By carrying God's ideas directly into our heart (see 2 Nephi 33:1), the Spirit enables us to bypass the barriers of imperfect language and thereby understand and feel the import of his teachings more fully.

DOCTRINE AND COVENANTS 19:11–12
What is "endless" or "eternal" punishment?

Elder James E. Talmage explained that "any punishment ordained of God is eternal, for He is eternal. His is a system of endless punishment, for it will always exist as a place or condition prepared for disobedient spirits; yet the infliction of the penalty will have an end in every case of acceptable repentance and reparation." The duration of these punishments "will be graded according to the sin" (*Articles of*

Faith, 60–61). Hence, God's system of punishment might be likened to a prison that continues to exist even though individual inmates come and go.

DOCTRINE AND COVENANTS 19:13, 20
Of what did Martin Harris need to repent?

Mr. Egbert B. Grandin, who was printing the Book of Mormon in Palmyra, New York, stopped work on the nearly completed project when a group of townspeople issued a resolution declaring that none of them would purchase the book. Anticipating such an action, Martin Harris had agreed to pay in advance the publication price of three thousand dollars. He was now reluctant to do so, and the Lord admonished him to honor his earlier commitment (see D&C 19:25–26, 34–35). Martin heeded the admonition, mortgaged his farm, and eventually sold 151 acres at a great sacrifice (see Backman and Cowan, *Joseph Smith and the Doctrine and Covenants,* 24–25).

DOCTRINE AND COVENANTS 19:18
What is the significance of this statement about the Savior's suffering?

The Savior's atoning sacrifice is the most important event in the history of our world. It is the necessary foundation for the gospel plan.

Elder Joseph Fielding Smith taught: "We get into the habit of thinking, I suppose, that his great suffering was when he was nailed to the cross by his hands and his feet and was left there to suffer until he died. As excruciating as that pain was, that was not the greatest suffering that he had to undergo, for in some way which I cannot understand, but which I accept on faith, and which you must accept on faith, he carried on his back the burden of the sins of the whole world . . . and so great was his suffering before he ever went to the cross, we are informed, that blood oozed from the pores of his body, and he prayed to his Father that the cup might pass if possible, but not being possible he was willing to drink" (in Conference Report, Oct. 1947, 147–48).

Some modern scholars have questioned whether Jesus actually bled from every pore. Doctrine and Covenants 19 confirms that the statements in the New Testament about the Savior's suffering are true.

DOCTRINE AND COVENANTS 19:25
Why was Martin Harris told not to seek his neighbor's life or his wife?

Available historical sources do not shed light on the specific circumstances behind this admonition.

DOCTRINE AND COVENANTS 19:27
How are the Lamanites a remnant of the Jews?

Even though the Lamanites' ancestor Lehi was of the tribe of Manasseh (see Alma 10:3), he and his family lived at Jerusalem, which was in the kingdom of Judah. They could therefore have been regarded as Jews by citizenship. Furthermore, the Lamanites were also descended from the "people of Zarahemla" who had accompanied Mulek from Jerusalem (Omni 1:13–19). {See D&C 3:17.} Hence, they also had the blood of Judah in their veins.

DOCTRINE AND COVENANTS 20:1
By what name was the Lord's Church to be known?

In Doctrine and Covenants 20, the Lord's Church is referred to as "the Church of Christ." Other elements were later added to the Church's official title. {See D&C 115:4.} Nevertheless, the title "The Church of Jesus Christ" remains preeminent. {See D&C 1:30.}

DOCTRINE AND COVENANTS 20:1
What do we know about the date of Jesus' birth, and why do we celebrate Christmas when we do?

Most biblical scholars agree that the Savior could not have been born in December because shepherds would not have been out at night with their flocks during that season of the year. Many suggest spring as a more probable time.

Evidence from the Book of Mormon confirms that Christ was born during the spring. The Nephites counted their years from the time when they saw the wondrous signs of his birth. Almost exactly thirty-three years later, on the fourth day of the first month in the thirty-fourth year, the sign of the Crucifixion was seen (see 3 Nephi 2:8; 8:5). This meant that the Lord was born and later died at the same time of year. The New Testament records that his crucifixion occurred at the time of the Passover, a Jewish holiday celebrated during the early spring. All this evidence points to the conclusion that Jesus Christ was born during the early spring and accords with the instructions in Doctrine and Covenants 20:1 that the Church should be organized on Tuesday, 6 April 1830, eighteen hundred and thirty years after the Savior had come in the flesh.

During the centuries after the Savior's birth, some Christians began to combine their celebration of that event with northern Europeans' observance of the winter solstice. Even though we know the Savior was born in April, it is appropriate to remember his life at any time of the year. Hence we join other Christians each December in celebrating the momentous event in Bethlehem.

DOCTRINE AND COVENANTS 20:9
How can the Book of Mormon contain "the fulness of the gospel"
when it does not discuss such important doctrines and practices
as baptism for the dead or eternal marriage?

On several occasions the Savior has defined what his gospel is—faith in his atoning sacrifice, repentance of sins, baptism by immersion, receiving the Holy Ghost, and enduring to the end (see 3 Nephi 27:13–22; D&C 33:10–12; 39:6; 76:40–42).

President Ezra Taft Benson explained that when the Lord spoke of the Book of Mormon as containing the "fulness of the gospel," he did not mean that "it contains every teaching, every doctrine ever revealed. Rather, it means that in the Book of Mormon we will find the fulness of those doctrines required for our salvation. And they are taught plainly and simply so that even children can learn the ways of salvation and exaltation" (*Ensign,* Nov. 1986, 6).

The Book of Mormon powerfully proclaims to honest readers the gospel's most fundamental principles, testified Elder Marion G. Romney. "From almost every page of the book, there will come to them a moving testimony that Jesus is indeed the Christ, the Son of the Living God, our Redeemer and Savior. This witness alone will be a sustaining anchor in every storm. In the Book of Mormon, they will find the plainest explanation of Christ's divine mission and atonement to be found anywhere in sacred writ. . . . Don't be content with what someone else says about what is in it. Drink deeply from the divine fountain itself" (in Conference Report, Apr. 1960, 112).

If we have faith in Jesus Christ, live basic gospel principles, and endure to the end—doctrines clearly taught in the Book of Mormon—

such other specific principles as baptism for the dead and eternal marriage would be (and now have been) made known to us.

DOCTRINE AND COVENANTS 20:28
How are the Father, the Son, and the Holy Ghost "one God"?

"Correctly interpreted, God in this sense means Godhead," taught President Joseph Fielding Smith (*Answers to Gospel Questions*, 2:142). The Father, the Son, and the Holy Ghost are one in purpose, glory, and power. The Savior prayed that we, too, might become one even as he and his Father are (see John 17:20–22).

DOCTRINE AND COVENANTS 20:30–32
How do justification, sanctification, and grace fit into the gospel plan?

Justification is a "judicial act" by which the Lord grants remission of sins, releasing the individual from the punishments required by justice—upon condition of faith, repentance, and baptism (Smith and Sjodahl, *Commentary*, 104). This "preparatory gospel" is administered by the lesser priesthood (see D&C 84:26–27), preparing us for the greater change of sanctification.

"To be sanctified," explained Elder Bruce R. McConkie, "is to become clean, pure, and spotless; to be free from the blood and sins of the world; to become a new creature of the Holy Ghost, one whose body has been renewed by the rebirth of the Spirit. Sanctification is a state of saintliness, a state attained only by conformity to the laws and ordinances of the gospel. The plan of salvation is the system and means provided whereby men may sanctify their souls and thereby become worthy of a celestial inheritance" (*Mormon Doctrine*, 675).

Grace is the "divine means of help or strength, given through the bounteous mercy and love of Jesus Christ" (LDS Bible Dictionary, 697).

DOCTRINE AND COVENANTS 20:37
Who are the parties to the covenant made at baptism?

We often speak of baptism as a covenant made between us and God, but we overlook that this verse, together with Alma's instructions (see Mosiah 18:8–10), clearly identifies the Church as another party to the baptismal covenant. A person who is converted and baptized truly does "join the Church." Candidates for baptism are to "witness before the church" that they are worthy to become members and that they are ready to "take upon them the name of Jesus Christ" and faithfully keep his commandments. Those who are baptized promise their fellow Church members that they will "bear one another's burdens . . . mourn with those who mourn . . . and comfort those who stand in need of comfort." They also promise to "stand as witnesses of God" in every aspect of their lives. God promises them remission, or forgiveness, of their sins and assures them that he will "pour out his Spirit more abundantly" upon them.

Notice how many of these commitments are specifically reflected in the sacramental prayers (see D&C 20:77, 79). In a very real sense we renew our baptismal covenants as we worthily and thoughtfully partake of the sacramental emblems each Sunday.

DOCTRINE AND COVENANTS 20:38–59
What do the titles of these priesthood offices mean?

Four priesthood offices functioned in the Church at the time of its organization. The title *deacon* comes from the Greek word *diakonos* which means "servant or messenger"; deacons traditionally have functioned in such serving roles as passing the sacrament, helping widows, and so forth. *Teacher* aptly describes the responsibility of one who is to watch over and expound the gospel to Church members. *Priest* is the title for the minimum office required to perform such priesthood ordinances as baptism, administering the sacrament, and ordinations to the Aaronic Priesthood. *Elder* is a form of the word *older* and denotes those who are more mature. Elders have a greater spiritual and leadership role than do bearers of the Aaronic priesthood; significantly, young men receive this office at about the age many societies consider to be the beginning of adulthood.

DOCTRINE AND COVENANTS 20:59
How can young deacons effectively "warn, expound, exhort, and teach, and invite all to come unto Christ"?

Paul counseled his young associate Timothy: "Let no man despise thy youth" (1 Timothy 4:12). Likewise today we should not minimize the good being done by faithful young men and young women. Elder Henry B. Eyring described how one young man returned to faithful activity when "the Savior had reached out through a twelve-year-old servant assigned by a thirteen-year-old quorum president" (*Ensign*, Nov. 1995, 38).

President Gordon B. Hinckley reminded the young bearers of the Aaronic Priesthood that they need to be worthy to teach and bless others effectively. He cautioned: "You cannot afford to partake of things that will weaken your minds and your bodies. These include cocaine, 'crack,' alcohol, tobacco. You cannot be involved in immoral activity. You cannot do these things and be valiant as warriors in the cause of the Lord in the great, everlasting contest that goes on for the souls of our Father's children" (*Ensign*, Nov. 1986, 44).

DOCTRINE AND COVENANTS 20:60
In what sense are brethren ordained "by the power of the Holy Ghost"?

A priesthood bearer performing ordinations or any other priesthood ordinances does so in the name of Jesus Christ. He should seek the guidance of the Spirit to know precisely what the Savior would have him do and say. The Fifth Article of Faith affirms that "we believe that a man must be called of God by prophecy." In other words, we believe that his calling should be a result of inspiration. Finally, the priesthood and power of the Holy Ghost are simply two manifestations of the same power—the power of God.

"I believe that when the Presidency of this Church nominates a person for an office, it is not a personal nomination," testified Elder Marion G. Romney. "I have that confidence in the Presidency and that testimony of the divinity of this Church. I believe that the Lord Jesus Christ reveals to them through the Spirit of the Holy Ghost the men they should name to office, and I believe that same spirit will inspire and direct the presidents of stakes and the bishops of wards and the heads of other organizations in this Church, if they will live for such inspiration, so that when they name people for office they will name them under the inspiration of the Holy Spirit" (in Conference Report, Oct. 1947, 40).

DOCTRINE AND COVENANTS 20:61
What schedules has the Church followed in holding conferences?

Early Latter-day Saints usually met in conferences every three months. Only after Church membership had become larger and more scattered did a distinction emerge between general conferences and stake conferences. By the late 1830s general conferences were usually held in April (to commemorate the anniversary of the Church's organization) and October. Missions around the world often scheduled their main conferences at these same two times. Over the years stake conferences were held quarterly, but in 1979 their frequency was cut to two per year. In more recent years these conferences have been supplemented by occasional multistake, regional, or area conferences.

DOCTRINE AND COVENANTS 20:63–64
What are certificates and licenses?

Certificates are documents stating that an ordinance such as baptism or ordination to an office in the priesthood has taken place. Licenses are authorizations for a person to act in a specific calling, such as serving as a missionary. Present-day examples of licenses are temple recommends and recommends to perform an ordinance, which may be used when a priesthood bearer performs an ordinance outside his own ward or branch.

DOCTRINE AND COVENANTS 20:65
What is our role in sustaining Church leaders?

"The Lord will call whom He sees proper to call to His priesthood," explained Elder B. H. Roberts, "but when in the exercise of the functions of the priesthood or its offices it comes to presiding over the Church or any of the branches or departments thereof, that can only be with the consent of those over whom they preside" (History of the Church, 5:522 n).

President J. Reuben Clark Jr. pointed out that "the power of 'nominating' or calling to office" resides with inspired leaders. "When the presiding authority has so 'nominated' or chosen, or called any man to office, that man is then presented to the body of the Church to be sustained, in political language 'elected'.

"Thus the body of the Church has no calling or 'nominating' power, but only the sustaining, or politically speaking, the 'electing' power" (in Conference Report, Oct. 1940, 28).

Even as the calling of individuals to office should be guided by inspiration, so should we seek the same Spirit as we exercise our right to sustain those who have been called (see D&C 26:2). President Joseph Fielding Smith counseled, "I have no right to raise my hand in opposition to a man who is appointed to any position in this Church, simply because I may not like him, or because of some personal dis-agreement or feeling I may have, but only on the grounds that he is guilty of wrong doing, of transgression of the laws of the Church which would disqualify him for the position which he is called to hold" (*Doctrines of Salvation*, 3:124).

"If a man be a teacher, and I vote that I will sustain him in his position," stressed President John Taylor, "when he visits me in an offi-cial capacity I will welcome him and treat him with consideration, kindness and respect and if I need counsel I will ask it at his hand, and I will do everything I can to sustain him. . . . And then if anybody in my presence were to whisper something about him disparaging to his reputation, I would say, Look here! are you a Saint? Yes. Did you not hold up your hand to sustain him? Yes. Then why do you not do it?" (in *Journal of Discourses*, 21:207).

DOCTRINE AND COVENANTS 20:66
What were "traveling bishops"?

Edward Partridge became the Church's first bishop in February 1831 (see D&C 41:9). Newel K. Whitney was called in December of that same year to be the second bishop. Bishop Whitney was given responsibility for the Saints in Ohio (see D&C 72), and Bishop Partridge was responsible for the Saints in Zion, or Missouri. Because the Saints were quite scattered, both bishops had to travel among sev-eral small congregations to perform their duties. Not until 1839, when the Saints settled in Nauvoo, were bishops associated with specific local congregations known as wards.

DOCTRINE AND COVENANTS 20:68
Shouldn't converts be instructed before they are baptized?

A casual reading of Doctrine and Covenants 20:68 may leave the impression that converts are to be taught about the Church after they are baptized and before they are confirmed, but a closer reading gives us a better understanding. Section 20 was revealed as a summary of the Church's teachings and practices for the benefit of prospective mem-bers. The italicized phrases in verses 37, 38, and 68 can be thought of as subheadings that precede major divisions. Hence the first part of verse 68, which is in italics, introduces the rest of section 20, which treats "the duty of the members after they are received by baptism." The remainder of verse 68, which is not in italics, states that converts are to be instructed before they are confirmed—and also before they are baptized.

DOCTRINE AND COVENANTS 20:73
What wording should be used in performing baptisms?

The words of the baptismal prayer revealed in the Doctrine and Covenants are slightly different from those in 3 Nephi 11:24–25, but the essential elements are identical. The variation may reflect differences between the Nephites' language and our own, or it may be that in the Book of Mormon the Savior was addressing brethren to whom he had personally given authority. In any case, we should use the wording revealed most recently and directly into our language—the version recorded in the Doctrine and Covenants.

DOCTRINE AND COVENANTS 20:76
Is the congregation required to kneel when the priest blesses the sacramental emblems?

With may also mean "in the presence of," so the revelation requires the priest, not necessarily the congregation, to kneel.

DOCTRINE AND COVENANTS 20:79
Why do we use water rather than wine in the sacrament?

At the time the Church was organized, wine was commonly used. Only a few months later, however, the Lord instructed that "it mattereth not" what emblems we use for the sacrament as long as we remember the Savior's body and blood. He specifically instructed Joseph Smith not to buy wine from those who might be the Saints' enemies (see D&C 27:2–4). Soon water became the most commonly used emblem. Though the red color of wine may remind us of the Savior's blood, water is also an appropriate symbol because it is essential to life and because its clearness reminds us of the Savior's cleansing power.

DOCTRINE AND COVENANTS 20:81–84
Why and how should membership records be kept?

Doctrine and Covenants 20:81–84 illustrate the point that procedures may change whereas principles remain constant. Moroni wrote that a record of members was maintained so that "they might be remembered and nourished" by the Church (Moroni 6:4). The procedure of representatives of the various branches personally exchanging membership records at conferences was suitable for the small 1830 Church. During the early twentieth century, the best procedure was for records to be sent to a membership department at Church headquarters whenever members moved from one ward or branch to another. More recently, computers have facilitated the Church's keeping its membership rolls up to date. Even more efficient means may emerge in the future, but the purpose will still be the same: to make Church leaders and members aware of those whom we may strengthen through gospel teaching and Church activity.

DOCTRINE AND COVENANTS 21
To whom was this revelation given?

Doctrine and Covenants 21, a revelation given at the meeting in which the Church was organized, seems to have been directed to at least three audiences: Joseph Smith (see v. 1), the Church (see v. 4), and Oliver Cowdery (see v. 10). Nevertheless, we should seek to apply the whole revelation to ourselves. Even though some sections of the Doctrine and Covenants are addressed to specific individuals (for example, sections 11 and 12 are addressed to Hyrum Smith and Joseph Knight Sr., respectively), the Lord emphasizes that he is speaking to all who have a desire to serve (see D&C 11:27; 12:7). He has declared, "What I say unto one I say unto all" (D&C 61:18, 36; 93:49).

DOCTRINE AND COVENANTS 21:1
What is the meaning of the titles to be applied to the president of the Church?

Joseph Smith was to be known by various titles, each of which shed light on a different facet of his calling.

Elder John A. Widtsoe explained that a *seer* is "one who sees with spiritual eyes. He perceives the meaning of that which seems obscure to others; therefore he is an interpreter and clarifier of eternal truth. He foresees the future from the past and the present. This he does by the power of the Lord operating through him directly, or indirectly with the aid of divine instruments such as the Urim and Thummim" (*Evidences and Reconciliations*, 258).

Joseph Smith was called a *translator* because of his assignment to translate the Book of Mormon by the gift and power of God. Within a few years he likewise translated the book of Abraham.

31

A *prophet* is God's messenger or spokesman, "one who speaks before or in behalf of another." Elder Widtsoe pointed out that "the principal business of a prophet has mistakenly been thought to foretell coming events, to utter prophecies, which is only one of the several prophetic functions.

"In the sense that a prophet is a man who receives revelations from the Lord, the titles 'seer and revelator' merely amplify the larger and inclusive meaning of the title 'prophet'" (*Evidences and Reconciliations,* 258).

An *apostle* is a "special witness of the name of Christ in all the world" (D&C 107:23). {See D&C 107:23.} "The title 'Apostle' is . . . one of special significance and sanctity," taught Elder James E. Talmage. "By derivation the word 'apostle' is the English equivalent of the Greek apostolos, indicating a messenger, an ambassador, or literally 'one who is sent.' It signifies that he who is rightly so called, speaks and acts not of himself, but as the representative of a higher power whence his commission issued; and in this sense the title is that of a servant, rather than that of a superior. . . .

" . . . So great is the sanctity of this special calling, that the title 'Apostle' should not be used lightly as the common or ordinary form of address" (*Jesus the Christ,* 228–29 n. 2).

Elder is the title of one who bears the Melchizedek Priesthood "whether the individuals concerned are or have been ordained to the office of elder or not" (McConkie, *Mormon Doctrine,* 215). The use of the title *elder,* explained President Joseph Fielding Smith, "makes it needless to use unnecessarily sacred terms as 'Apostle,' 'Patriarch,' 'High Priest,' etc. It is proper in general usage to speak of the apostles, the seventies and all others holding the Melchizedek Priesthood as 'elders.' Of course, the term President, in speaking of the First Presidency, is the proper designation" (*Church History and Modern Revelation,* 1:95).

DOCTRINE AND COVENANTS 22
What is the "new and everlasting covenant," and what are the "old covenants" and "dead works" it superseded?

We often associate the phrase "new and everlasting covenant" with the covenant of eternal marriage, but it is actually far broader than that. It is the gospel of Jesus Christ (see D&C 66:2): "new" because it had just been restored and "everlasting" in its blessings.

"Every principle, key and authority, belonging to the Gospel of Jesus Christ," wrote President Joseph Fielding Smith, "constitute the new and 'everlasting covenant.' It is not, as some may believe, any one covenant which is everlasting, but the sum total of them all" (*Church History and Modern Revelation*, 1:244–45).

Elder Bruce R. McConkie distinguished between marriage, which is *a* new and everlasting covenant, and the gospel as a whole, which is *the* new and everlasting covenant (see *Mormon Doctrine*, 529–30).

The revelation recorded in section 22 was received when individuals questioned the need to be baptized again. The phrases "old covenants" and "dead works" referred to their earlier baptisms, which were not valid because they were performed without priesthood authority.

INSTRUCTIONS
TO EARLY LABORERS

DOCTRINE AND COVENANTS 23 THROUGH 40

The revelations recorded in Doctrine and Covenants 23 through 40 were given during 1830 and 1831 after the Church was organized and had begun expanding its ministry in New York and Pennsylvania. In these sections we meet more early leaders of the Restoration, including Parley and Orson Pratt, Sidney Rigdon, and Edward Partridge. Through these revelations the knowledge of more doctrines and practices were unfolded to the Saints.

DOCTRINE AND COVENANTS 23:3
What did the Lord mean when he told Hyrum Smith that his duty was "unto the church forever" because of his family?

The Lord told Hyrum and his father that it was their calling to strengthen the Church forever (see D&C 23:3, 5). "This could not refer to their personal ministry on Earth, but it has been fulfilled in the ministry of their descendants, and will, no doubt, come true, as the Revelations say, 'forever'" (Smith and Sjodahl, *Commentary*, 122). President Joseph Fielding Smith believed that this promise to the Smiths referred especially to their descendants holding the hereditary office of patriarch to the Church (see *Doctrines of Salvation*, 3:164).

DOCTRINE AND COVENANTS 23:6–7
Why was Joseph Knight not told that his sins were forgiven?

The other four individuals addressed in this revelation had already been baptized and were assured that their sins were forgiven. Joseph Knight Sr., on the other hand, was directed to join the Church by being baptized, which he did the following June. Before he received this ordinance he could not qualify for the remission of his sins.

34

DOCTRINE AND COVENANTS 24:3
What does it mean to "magnify thine office"?

Magnify means to enlarge, to make our calling more important because of the service we render to others. {See **D&C 84:33–41**.} Joseph Smith was specifically instructed to spend his full time in Church service and to forsake temporal labors (see D&C 24:7, 9). He was therefore promised that the Church would provide the support he and his family needed. {See **D&C 42:70–73**.}

DOCTRINE AND COVENANTS 24:15
What is the meaning of the phrase "casting off the dust of your feet"?

The Lord has always instructed his people to share the gospel. Among the Nephites, Jacob and Joseph took this responsibility seriously: "We did magnify our office unto the Lord, taking upon us the responsibility, answering the sins of the people upon our own heads if we did not teach them the word of God with all diligence" (Jacob 1:18–19). The Master directed his ancient apostles to shake the dust off their feet when their message was rejected (see Matthew 10:14). The dust represented the sins of the people, and this act symbolized that the missionaries had faithfully discharged their responsibility, so that the burden of the sins of these people was off their shoulders. Jacob, for example, when he had finished teaching his people, shook off his garments, declaring that he had shaken their "iniquities from [his] soul" (2 Nephi 9:44).

When Paul was rejected at Corinth, he likewise "shook his raiment, and said unto them, Your blood be upon your own heads; I am clean" (Acts 18:6). This ritual, primarily for the benefit of the missionary, was normally to be performed in private (see D&C 60:15).

"The missionaries of the Church who faithfully perform their duty," explained President Joseph Fielding Smith, "are under the obligation of leaving their testimony with all with whom they come in contact in their work. This testimony will stand as a witness against those who reject the message, at the judgment" (*Church History and Modern Revelation,* 1:223).

DOCTRINE AND COVENANTS 24:18
What does it mean to go without scrip or staves?

Scrip means "a small bag" or "wallet" or may refer to such substitutes for money as a bank certificate or share of stock (Webster, *American Dictionary*). *Staves* is an archaic plural of *staff.* These two items symbolize material preparation. In the early days of the Church, missionaries sometimes traveled "without purse or scrip," typically in rural areas, depending on the blessings of the Lord and the generosity of the people for food and lodging. In the present day, however, missionary work has increasingly shifted into urban areas. Vagrancy laws and other conditions have made the former practice impossible. President Charles W. Penrose acknowledged that he had performed all his missionary work "without purse or scrip" but added, "Now I do not say that this should be done now. I believe that as circumstances change, the Lord changes his commandments, to correspond therewith" (in Conference Report, Oct. 1921, 17).

DOCTRINE AND COVENANTS 25:1
In what unique sense was Emma a daughter of God?

The Savior reminded Emma that "all those who receive [and live] my gospel are sons and daughters in my kingdom." {See D&C 11:30.}

Elder Bruce R. McConkie taught: "All women are the daughters of God because of their pre-existent birth as female spirits. However, the designation *daughters of God,* as used in the revelations, has a far more pointed meaning than this. Just as men who pursue a steadfast course toward exaltation become the sons of God while in this life, so women who walk hand-in-hand in obedience with them become the daughters of God. (D&C 25:1; 76:24; Mosiah 5:7.)

"The temple ordinances, including celestial marriage, precede attainment of that membership in the household of God which makes one a daughter. Those who are adopted as daughters in this life will, if they continue faithful, gain exaltation in the world to come" (*Mormon Doctrine,* 179–80).

DOCTRINE AND COVENANTS 25:3
What is the meaning of Emma's being an "elect lady"?

Elect means "chosen" (Webster, *American Dictionary*) and is often used in connection with those who have qualified for exaltation in the celestial kingdom. In 1842, when the Relief Society was organized at Nauvoo, Joseph Smith referred to his wife's being an "elect lady" and explained that "elect meant to be elected to a certain work. &c., and that the revelation was then fulfilled by Sister Emma's election to the Presidency of the Society" (*History of the Church*, 4:552–53). {See D&C 25:7.}

DOCTRINE AND COVENANTS 25:5–8
How do the instructions to Emma Smith shed light on the role of women today?

The first responsibility the Lord spoke of in this revelation to Emma Smith was to be a good wife to her husband (see D&C 25:5–6). Our latter-day prophets consistently have emphasized a woman's key role in the home. For example, President Harold B. Lee declared: "We say the prime role in life for a woman is to become a wife and a mother" ("Be Loyal to the Royal within You," 93).

Our prophets have just as strongly emphasized that a man's key role is also in the home. "Mothers play an important role as the heart of the home," declared President Ezra Taft Benson, "but this in no way lessens the equally important role fathers should play, as head of the home, in nurturing, training, and loving their children" (in Conference Report, Oct. 1987, 62). Speaking in a priesthood session of general conference, President Lee told the priesthood bearers, "The greatest of the Lord's work you brethren will ever do as fathers will be within the walls of your own home" (in Conference Report, Apr. 1973, 130). In another often-quoted statement, President David O. McKay affirmed, "No other success can compensate for failure in the home" (in Conference Report, Apr. 1964, 5).

A woman's role is not limited to the home, however. The Lord also assigned Emma Smith to serve in the Church and counseled her to devote more time to learning and writing (see D&C 25:7–8, 11). Elder Bruce R. McConkie taught: "A married woman's place is in the home, where she sustains and supports her husband; a woman's place is in the Church, where she expounds scripture, writes wise documents, and learns much; a woman's place is out rendering compassionate service to her fellow beings, in and out of the Church, a woman's place is in preaching the gospel and doing missionary work; her calling is to do good and work righteousness in every place and under all circumstances" (*Ensign*, Jan. 1979, 63).

DOCTRINE AND COVENANTS 25:7
Why does this verse say that Emma would be "ordained"?

A dictionary published about the time of this revelation indicates that although the principal meaning of *ordain* is "to invest with a ministerial function or sacerdotal [priestly] power," the word also may mean "to set apart for an office; to appoint" (Webster, *American Dictionary*).

"The term 'ordain' was used generally in the early days of the Church in reference to both ordination and setting apart," explained President Joseph Fielding Smith. "Men holding the Priesthood were said to have been 'ordained' to preside over branches and to perform special work. Sisters also were said to have been 'ordained' when they were called to some special duty or responsibility. In later years we developed a distinction between ordain and setting apart. . . . This saying that Emma Smith was 'ordained' to expound scripture, does not mean that she had conferred upon her the Priesthood, but that she was set apart to this calling, which found its fulfillment in the Relief Society of the Church" (*Church History and Modern Revelation,* 1:126).

President John Taylor later recalled the organization of the Relief Society: "the Prophet called Sister Emma to be an elect lady." {See D&C 25:3.} "In compliance with Brother Joseph's request I set her apart, and also ordained . . . her counselors. Some of the sisters have thought that these sisters mentioned were, in this ordination, ordained to the Priesthood. And for the information of all interested in this subject I will say, it is not the calling of these sisters to hold the Priesthood, only in connection with their husbands, they being one with their husbands" (in *Journal of Discourses,* 21:367–68).

DOCTRINE AND COVENANTS 25:12
How can music affect us for good or ill?

The First Presidency said: "Inspirational music is an essential part of our church meetings. The hymns invite the Spirit of the Lord, create a feeling of reverence, unify us as members, and provide a way for us to offer praises to the Lord.

"Some of the greatest sermons are preached by the singing of hymns. Hymns move us to repentance and good works, build testimony and faith, comfort the weary, console the mourning, and inspire us to endure to the end" (*Hymns,* 1985, ix).

"As we sing we should think about the messages of the words,"

Elder Dallin H. Oaks taught. "Our hymns contain matchless doctrinal sermons, surpassed only by the scriptures in their truth and poetic impact" (in Conference Report, Oct. 1994, 12).

Elder Boyd K. Packer warned the youth of the Church especially that music may also have negative influences on us: "You cannot afford to fill your mind with the unworthy hard music of our day. It is *not* harmless. It can welcome onto the stage of your mind unworthy thoughts and set the tempo to which they dance and to which you may act.

"You degrade yourself when you identify with all of those things which seem now to surround such extremes in music: the shabbiness, the irreverence, the immorality, and the addictions. Such music as that is not worthy of you" (in Conference Report, Oct. 1973, 25).

DOCTRINE AND COVENANTS 26:2
How can we vote meaningfully when given the opportunity in Church meetings?

In the world, we are encouraged to study issues and candidates thoroughly before casting our vote. In the Church, we vote immediately when names are presented. To vote meaningfully we must be prepared spiritually so that we can be guided by the Spirit of the Lord (see D&C 26:2; 28:13).

"It may seem rather a dry and formal matter to some of the people to come together and lift up their hands to sustain the authorities of the Church," said Elder Charles W. Penrose, "but it is a necessary duty and, if we look at it properly, we shall take pleasure therein. . . . it was designed by the Almighty in the organization of this Church, that the voice of the people should respond to the voice of the Lord. It is the voice of the Lord and the voice of the people together in this Church that sanctions all things therein" (in *Journal of Discourses*, 21:45).

Elder Bruce R. McConkie asserted: "The Church (or kingdom) is not a democracy; legislation is not enacted by the body of people composing the organization; they do not make the laws governing themselves. The Church is a kingdom. The Lord Jesus Christ is the Eternal King, and the President of the Church, the mouthpiece of God on earth, is the earthly king. All things come to the Church from the King of the kingdom in heaven, through the king of the kingdom on earth. There is, of course, the democratic principle of common consent whereunder the people may accept or reject what the Lord offers to them. Acceptance brings salvation; rejection leads to damnation" (*Mormon Doctrine*, 416).

DOCTRINE AND COVENANTS 27:2–4
Why don't we use wine in the sacrament?

After the Lord cautioned against buying wine from "enemies," and particularly after the Word of Wisdom (D&C 89) was revealed in 1833, the Church used water in the sacrament. President Brigham Young acknowledged that in biblical times people typically drank wine but emphasized that this was done because "they were not blessed so profusely as we are with the crystal streams from the mountains" (in *Journal of Discourses*, 19:92). Water is an appropriate emblem of Christ's cleansing blood. {See D&C 20:79.}

DOCTRINE AND COVENANTS 27:6–7
Who is Elias?

The name or title *Elias* is used in the scriptures in at least three different senses.

First, Elias and Elijah are two forms of the same name, the former coming from the Greek and the latter from the Hebrew. Many references to Elias in the New Testament actually refer to Elijah. For example, it was Elijah who appeared with Moses on the Mount of Transfiguration (see Matthew 17:1–3). Joseph Smith used the two forms of this name in his discussion of the powers of the Aaronic and Melchizedek Priesthoods (see *Teachings of the Prophet Joseph Smith*, 335–41).

Second, *Elias* is the title of an individual messenger or forerunner, or of a group of persons sent to prepare the way (see Matthew 17:11). Perhaps John the Baptist is the best known of those who have come in the role of an Elias (see Luke 1:17). Doctrine and Covenants 27:6 uses *Elias* both as a general title and as a specific title of John the Baptist.

Three, *Elias* was a great prophet who lived in the days of Abraham. This prophet appeared in the Kirtland Temple in 1836 and restored the "dispensation of the gospel of Abraham" (D&C 110:12). {See D&C 110:12.}

DOCTRINE AND COVENANTS 28:1–7
Who may receive revelation in the Church?

When Moses was told that certain individuals were prophesying, allegedly without authority, he replied that he wished all of God's people could be prophets (see Numbers 11:26–29). Similarly, all Latter-day Saints may receive revelation in answer to their prayers but only concerning their stewardship—each of us for our own lives, parents for their family, bishops for their ward members, and so forth. Only the prophet is entitled to receive revelation for the whole Church.

Elder Spencer W. Kimball instructed: "While inspiration and even revelation is available to every individual for himself, to every head of family for his family, to every bishop for his ward, to every stake president for his stake, yet none of these will receive revelations for the Church, and any revelations they receive for themselves will always parallel and never counter the major revelations to the prophets of the Lord" (*That You May Not Be Deceived,* 9).

In 1913 the First Presidency declared: "When visions, dreams, tongues, prophecy, impressions or any extraordinary gift or inspiration, convey something out of harmony with the accepted revelations of the Church or contrary to the decisions of its constituted authorities, Latter-day Saints may know that it is not of God, no matter how plausible it may appear. Also, they should understand that directions for the guidance of the Church will come, by revelation, through the head" (Joseph F. Smith, Anthon H. Lund, and Charles W. Penrose, *Improvement Era,* Sept. 1913, 1148–49).

DOCTRINE AND COVENANTS 28:8
What did the mission to the Lamanites accomplish?

Oliver Cowdery was the first to be called to "go unto the Lamanites" (D&C 28:8). Peter Whitmer Jr., Parley P. Pratt, and Ziba Peterson were soon called to the same work (see D&C 30:5–6; 32:1–4). These missionaries left Fayette, New York, late in October 1830. They first visited the Catteraugus Indians near Buffalo, where they left copies of the Book of Mormon. Thus the first formal mission of the Church carried the message of the restored gospel to the Lamanites and gave them the record of their fathers.

In Church history, however, the primary importance of this mission was not in its work with the Indians. Parley P. Pratt wanted to take the Book of Mormon to his old friend Sidney Rigdon, who was a leading minister in the Campbellite movement (a forerunner of the Disciples of Christ Church), at Mentor, near Kirtland, Ohio. Many future Church leaders were converted as a result of this visit, and by the following spring, there were about one thousand members of the Church in the area.

Meanwhile, the missionaries continued their journey west during the winter of 1830–31. Because of sectarian jealousy, the Latter-day Saint missionaries were expelled from among the Native Americans west of the Missouri River, but they were successful in converting many non-Indians in the vicinity of Independence, Missouri. By the spring of 1831, therefore, there were sizable Church congregations in Kirtland and in Independence—two centers that would play important roles in subsequent Church history.

DOCTRINE AND COVENANTS 28:11–13
Why was the Lord's counsel to Hiram Page given through Oliver Cowdery?

Oliver Cowdery and Hiram Page were good friends who became brothers-in-law when both married daughters of Peter Whitmer Sr. Because Oliver had supported Hiram's claim to have received revelations for the Church, he might have been more inclined to accept correction from Oliver. Furthermore, Oliver learned proper Church procedures as he was instructing his friend.

"It was very necessary that Oliver Cowdery should receive this admonition," explained President Joseph Fielding Smith, "for he was inclined to take issue with the Prophet even in regard to matters of revelation. Much good came out of this unpleasant incident, for the members were taught that there was order in the Church and only one appointed to receive commandments and revelations for their guidance, and he was the one God had called" (*Church History and Modern Revelation*, 1:135).

DOCTRINE AND COVENANTS 29:7–8
Why are we no longer asked to gather into one place?

Initially the need was for the Saints to gather in one central place in order to have a strong nucleus from which the Church's influence could be radiated. The Saints could thereby strengthen one another and more directly enjoy the Prophet's personal influence.

Nonetheless, revelations in the Doctrine and Covenants

(101:20–22; 115:17–18) anticipated the time when multiple gathering places would be established. Beginning in the 1890s and continuing into the twentieth century, the First Presidency directed people to stay in their homelands and build up the Church there. In 1921, for example, a *Millennial Star* editorial instructed: "The counsel of the General Authorities to the yet ungathered saints is not to flock Zionward under existing conditions; but to remain in the countries where they now dwell. . . . Such as have homes and employment, especially, should stay and help build up the Lord's work in the various missions and conferences and branches, strengthening the hands of the elders and other missionaries labouring among them" (Sept. 15, 1921, 585).

More than two thousand stakes have been established as gathering places worldwide. Not only are they places of refuge, but through their organization the Saints are better able to share the gospel with others by precept and example (see D&C 115:5–6). At the 1972 Mexico City Area Conference, Elder Bruce R. McConkie proclaimed: "The place of gathering for the Mexican Saints is in Mexico; the place of gathering for the Guatemalan Saints is in Guatemala; the place of gathering for the Brazilian Saints is in Brazil; and so it goes throughout the length and breadth of the whole earth. . . . every nation is the gathering place for its own people" (in Mexico and Central America Area Conference Report, 1972, 45).

At an area conference in Stockholm, Sweden, two years later, President Spencer W. Kimball counseled: "There is good reason for members of the Church who are isolated from the stakes and their benefits that they may wish to consider moving to central places, where all the blessings of the Church are available. Sometimes, of course, that is not feasible, and so we remain in the outskirts and build up the Church wherever we are. . . . Migration to America is not necessary any longer" (in Denmark, Finland, Norway, and Sweden Area Conference Report, 1974, 6).

Just before the Lord's second coming, there will once again be a need for the Saints to gather in one place to establish the center stake of Zion. In 1948, Elder Harold B. Lee cautioned: "The Lord has placed the responsibility for directing the work of gathering in the hands of the leaders of the Church to whom he will reveal his will where and when such gatherings would take place in the future. It would be well—before the frightening events concerning the fulfillment of all God's promises and predictions are upon us, that the Saints in every land prepare themselves and look forward to the instruction that shall come to them from the First Presidency of this Church as to where they shall be gathered and not be disturbed in their feelings until such instruction is given to them as it is revealed by the Lord to the proper authority" (in Conference Report, Apr. 1948, 55).

DOCTRINE AND COVENANTS 29:12
Will Judas help to judge us?

"We have every reason to expect," wrote Elder Bruce R. McConkie, "that the saints and the world will be judged by the apostles and prophets sent to carry the message of salvation to them; and that the great hierarchal chain of judgment with Christ at the head, will include Adam and the prophets of all ages, Peter and the apostles of all ages, and all the elders of the kingdom of all ages who have kept their covenants" (*Mormon Doctrine*, 399).

Judas, however, will not be part of this great system of judges. He lost his standing among the Twelve and was replaced by Matthias (see Acts 1:25–26).

DOCTRINE AND COVENANTS 29:32
What is the meaning of "first spiritual then temporal" and "first temporal then spiritual"?

Temporal, like *temporary*, comes from the Latin *temporis*, "pertaining to time." An 1828 dictionary defines this term as "pertaining to this life or this world"; it is opposed to that which is "spiritual concerns, which are far more important" (Webster, *American Dictionary*).

The scriptures teach that God created all things, including his own children, "spiritually, before they were naturally upon the face of the earth" (Moses 3:5). If we look back toward the beginning, we see that all things were "spiritual" before they became "temporal." After we leave this present life, we are taken into the spirit world. Even after the resurrection, our bodies of flesh and bone will be "spiritual" in character. "But they will not be blood bodies," Elder Joseph Fielding Smith clarified. "They will no longer be quickened by blood but quickened by the spirit which is eternal and they shall become immortal and shall never die" (in Conference Report, Apr. 1917, 63). If we look forward toward the end, we see that after our present "temporal" existence we will once again enter conditions that can best be described as "spiritual." Thus that which is "spiritual" is most enduring.

DOCTRINE AND COVENANTS 29:34
Isn't the Word of Wisdom a "temporal commandment"?

Living the principles set forth in Doctrine and Covenants 89 obviously brings temporal blessings (see D&C 89:2). Nevertheless, the essence of this commandment is spiritual. Through compliance with this law, we learn the great spiritual principle of obedience. As we take care of our mortal body, it becomes a more fit instrument through which our spirit can operate. As we suppress our physical appetites, we give greater relative emphasis to our spirit.

"In our mortal, or carnal, way of thinking," explained President Joseph Fielding Smith, "many of the commandments the Lord has required seem to be temporal." But "the Lord does not think in temporal terms; his plan is to bring to pass the immortality and eternal life of man. In his eyes, therefore, all the commandments that have to do with our present welfare, are considered to be but steps on the way to his eternal salvation" (*Church History and Modern Revelation,* 1:307–8).

DOCTRINE AND COVENANTS 29:46
Who is speaking in this revelation?

"In giving revelations," explained President Joseph Fielding Smith, "our Savior speaks at times for himself; at other times for the Father, and in the Father's name, as though he were the Father, and yet it is Jesus Christ, our Redeemer who gives the message. So, we see, in Doctrine and Covenants 29:1, that he introduces himself as 'Jesus Christ, your Redeemer,' but in the closing part of the revelation [v. 46] he speaks for the Father, and in the Father's name as though he were the Father, and yet it is still Jesus who is speaking, for the Father has put his name on him for that purpose" (*Doctrines of Salvation,* 1:27–28).

In 1916 the First Presidency declared: "In all His dealings with the human family Jesus the Son has represented and yet represents Elohim His Father in power and authority. . . . Thus the Father placed His name upon the Son; and Jesus Christ spoke and ministered in and through the Father's name; and so far as power, authority and Godship are concerned His words and acts were and are those of the Father" (in Clark, *Messages of the First Presidency,* 5:31–32).

DOCTRINE AND COVENANTS 30:9
What is suggested by the directive to proclaim the gospel "as with the voice of a trump"?

The image of a trumpet calls to mind a herald proclaiming his message so all can hear. In his preface to the Doctrine and Covenants, the Lord described his message as a "voice of warning" that all should prepare "for that which is to come, for the Lord is nigh" (D&C 1:4, 12). The directive to teach the gospel "as with the voice of a trump" requires us to proclaim it boldly and reminds us what our emphasis should be.

DOCTRINE AND COVENANTS 31:4
What is the significance of the Lord's saying that the field is "already to be burned"?

Earlier the Lord had said the field was "white already to harvest" (D&C 4:4), but now it has reached a more advanced state when it must be burned. {See D&C 4:4.} "After the long night of apostasy," wrote President Joseph Fielding Smith, "the world was filled with tradition, false doctrine and practice" (*Church History and Modern Revelation*, 1:36). The Lord's reference to the "eleventh hour" (D&C 33:3) and his repeated warning, "I come quickly" (D&C 33:18; 34:12; 35:27; 39:24), should heighten our sense of urgency to become involved in God's work.

DOCTRINE AND COVENANTS 31:10
How was Thomas B. Marsh a "physician" to the Church?

A dictionary published about the time of this revelation described a physician as "a person skilled in the art of healing; one whose profession is to prescribe remedies for diseases" (Webster, *American Dictionary*). The secondary definition may have applied even more directly: "In a spiritual sense, one that heals moral diseases; as a physician of the soul." In several instances Brother Marsh helped to resolve difficulties among the Saints. Historian A. Gary Anderson concluded: "These first recorded acts as a healer within the Church illustrate an ability in leadership and chronicle the fulfillment of his revelatory calling as 'physician'" ("Thomas B. Marsh," 139).

46

DOCTRINE AND COVENANTS 33:10–12
What exactly is the "gospel"?

Our word *gospel* comes from the Old English word *godspel,* mean-ing "good news." Even though the gospel embraces all truth, the Savior himself has outlined its core in at least four places (see 3 Nephi 27:13–22; D&C 33:10–12; 39:6; 76:40–42).

"The gospel can be viewed from two perspectives," President Ezra Taft Benson pointed out. "In the broadest sense, the gospel embraces all truth, all light, all revealed knowledge to mankind. In a more restrictive sense, the gospel means the doctrine of the Fall, the conse-quences of the fall of man that brought into the world physical and spiritual death, the atonement of Jesus Christ which brings to pass immortality and eternal life, and the ordinances of salvation" (*Teachings of Ezra Taft Benson,* 30).

The heart of the gospel message is that through Christ's atonement we can overcome our sins and return once again into God's presence. Hence the gospel has been described as "glad tidings" (D&C 19:29).

DOCTRINE AND COVENANTS 33:11
What is the baptism of fire?

"The Holy Ghost is a sanctifier," explained Elder Bruce R. McConkie, "and those who receive the baptism of fire have sin and evil burned out of their souls as though by fire" (*Mortal Messiah,* 2:50).

DOCTRINE AND COVENANTS 33:14
What are "the church articles and covenants"?

The "church articles and covenants" consisted of what we now know as Doctrine and Covenants 20 and 22. At the first conference of the Church, held at Fayette, New York, on 9 June 1830, the "Articles and Covenants [were] read by Joseph Smith Jr., and received by unan-imous vote of the whole congregation" (minutes taken by Oliver Cowdery; in Cannon and Cook, *Far West Record,* 1). The "Articles and Covenants" were an early guide for Church doctrines and procedures and thus were referred to at many Church meetings. They may be regarded as a forerunner to the later books of published revelations.

DOCTRINE AND COVENANTS 34:3
How does this verse expand our understanding
of the often-quoted "beloved" passage in John 3:16?

The passage in the Bible speaks of the great love God has for mankind, which led him to give his Only Begotten Son so that all might have eternal life. The revelation in Doctrine and Covenants 34 indicates that the Son shared this great love and thus was willing to endure the suffering required to accomplish his atoning sacrifice. We owe a great debt of gratitude to both the Father and the Son for the marvelous gift of the Atonement.

DOCTRINE AND COVENANTS 35:3
How does the Lord regard the work being done by other churches?

In Doctrine and Covenants 35 the Lord assured Sidney Rigdon, a Campbellite minister, that He knew his deeds and was now calling him to a "greater work" (v. 3). The Lord told James Covill, a Baptist minister, essentially the same thing in a later revelation (see D&C 39:7, 11). Evidently the Master regarded the previous service of these two clergymen as a "great work." Still, with the priesthood and a knowledge of the fulness of the gospel, they could do more. {See D&C 1:30.}

DOCTRINE AND COVENANTS 35:4
How did Sidney Rigdon prepare the way for the restored gospel?

Sidney Rigdon was a prominent minister in the Campbellite movement, which emphasized the need for a restoration of New Testament Christianity. Even though the Campbellites believed that could be accomplished simply by studying and following the pattern set forth in the Bible, Sidney Rigdon and his congregation were receptive to the Latter-day Saint missionaries' testimony that heavenly messengers had brought the ancient gospel and priesthood to earth once again.

DOCTRINE AND COVENANTS 35:20
To what scriptural work does this verse refer?

The Prophet's inspired version of the Bible is generally referred to as the Joseph Smith Translation (JST). It is not a translation in the usual sense because no foreign-language texts were involved. The Prophet received through revelation revisions that clarified the meaning of the King James Bible, sometimes correcting errors or restoring material that had been lost. The Joseph Smith Translation is more than a commentary on biblical passages. It is a clarifying restoration of the original scriptural message, or, more strictly speaking, an inspired English translation of that original message.

This project of translation began when the Prophet received the book of Moses by revelation between June 1830 and February 1831. By September of 1830, he had started his work of revising the Old Testament. In the following March, the Lord directed the Prophet to work on the New Testament (see D&C 45:60–61). He completed this phase of the project by 2 February 1833. About a month later, the Lord spoke to the Prophet about finishing "the translation of the prophets," that is, the Old Testament (see D&C 90:13) and counseled him not to revise the Apocrypha (see D&C 91). On 2 July 1833, Joseph Smith recorded: "We this day finished the translating of the Scriptures, for which we returned gratitude to our Heavenly Father" (*History of the Church,* 1:368).

The revisions in the Joseph Smith Translation help clarify biblical passages and gospel doctrines. The changes are most numerous in the books of Genesis and Matthew. Because the revisions were given by inspiration, this version is a most valuable work to study.

Joseph Smith's translation of the Bible contributes to our knowledge of gospel doctrines in still another way. The Prophet's questions about biblical passages led to several revelations now in the Doctrine and Covenants: sections 74, 76, 77, 86, 91, 93, 113, and 132. The Church included the most significant changes in the Joseph Smith Translation in the footnotes and appendix of the LDS edition of the King James Version of the Bible, first published in 1979 (see Matthews, *"A Plainer Translation"*).

DOCTRINE AND COVENANTS 38:1–4
Is Jesus Christ the same person as the God of the Old Testament?

Some students of the Bible erroneously view the God of the Old Testament as harsh and vindictive and so conclude that he cannot be the same person as Jesus Christ who taught the gospel of love. Doctrine and Covenants 38 clearly identifies the Savior as the one who created the world, dealt with the Prophet Enoch, and was known by Moses as "I Am." A comparison of the Old and the New Testament confirms that Jehovah is the same person as Jesus Christ. For example, Jehovah and Jesus Christ are identified as the Creator (Isaiah 45:11–12 and John 1:1–3, 14), as our only Savior (Isaiah 43:3, 11 and Acts 4:10–12), and as our Judge (Psalm 96:13 and John 5:22).

A careful reading of the Old Testament reveals God's tender mercies in the early dispensations. He was anxious to bless the obedient (see Deuteronomy 28), and he was likened to a loving shepherd (see Psalm 23; Isaiah 40:10–11). The commandment to love our neighbor is found not only in the New Testament but also in the record of Moses (see Leviticus 19:18).

DOCTRINE AND COVENANTS 38:2
If God knows all things, can we really be free?

When we are told that God knows what will happen in the future, we may wonder if we really have the power to influence future events through our present choices and actions. A parent may come to know his child so well that he can accurately predict what the child will choose to do in a given set of circumstances, but the parent's knowledge in no way determines the child's choices. And because parents' knowledge is less than perfect, they may be surprised by their children's choices. God's knowledge of his children, however, is perfect. Still, his foreknowledge of what we will do in no way causes us to do it. He has made us free to make choices and then to be accountable for them.

THE GATHERING IN OHIO

DOCTRINE AND COVENANTS 41 THROUGH 51

The mission to the Lamanites provided the Church's first contact with Ohio, where more Doctrine and Covenants revelations were received than in any other state. {See **D&C 28:8**.} Near the end of 1830, the Saints in New York and Pennsylvania were directed to move to "the Ohio" (D&C 37–38). Joseph Smith was one of the first to comply, arriving on a wintry 1 February 1831. During the next four months, as the Saints were gathering to Ohio, the revelations recorded in sections 41 through 51 brought forth such developments as the appointment of the first bishop. He administered the law of consecration, which was given in the revelation recorded in section 42 and in subsequent revelations.

DOCTRINE AND COVENANTS 41:7
Why was the Church to build a house for Joseph Smith?

Because the Prophet was expected to devote all his time to the Church, building him a house was one practical way the Saints could provide for his needs. {See **D&C 42:70–73**.}

DOCTRINE AND COVENANTS 42:11
Why is having recognized authority essential in the Church?

The need for priesthood authority is well understood, and Doctrine and Covenants 42 emphasizes that such authority must be acknowledged by the Church. The wisdom of the Lord's counsel has been demonstrated on various occasions over the years when apostates have arrived at Church headquarters claiming a commission—commission—known only to them—to take over. The falsity of their claims has been exposed by the fact that their supposed ordination was not "known to the church."

DOCTRINE AND COVENANTS 42:12–13
What should be the sources of our gospel teaching?

Three main sources of gospel knowledge should guide what we teach. First is the written scriptures. Doctrine and Covenants 42 specifically refers to the Bible and the Book of Mormon—the two standard works then in existence. That latter-day revelations should also be considered is evidenced in the reference to "the covenants and church articles," a forerunner to the Book of Commandments and the Doctrine and Covenants. {See D&C 33:14.}

Second, our teaching should "be directed by the Spirit" because the Holy Ghost is a revealer of truth. {See D&C 42:14.}

Third, though it is not specifically mentioned in this passage, our teaching should also be guided by the words of our living prophets. {See D&C 52:9.}

DOCTRINE AND COVENANTS 42:14
Why is it so essential to teach by the Spirit?

It is essential to teach by the Spirit because we want to teach the truth, and the Holy Ghost enables us to know what is true (see John 14:26; Moroni 10:5). Furthermore, the Spirit powerfully carries our teaching of the truth into the hearts of those who hear us (see 2 Nephi 33:1).

Three months after the revelation in Doctrine and Covenants 42 was given, the Lord again emphasized the importance of teaching by the Spirit: "If it be by some other way it is not of God" (D&C 50:18). "Now, what is the other way to teach than by the Spirit?" asked Elder Bruce R. McConkie. His answer: "Well, obviously, it is by the power of the intellect.

"Intellectual things—reason and logic—can do some good, and they can prepare the way, and they can get the mind ready to receive the spirit under certain circumstances. But conversion comes and the truth sinks into the hearts of people only when it is taught by the power of the Spirit" ("The Foolishness of Teaching," quoted in Millet and Dahl, *Capstone*, 51–52).

DOCTRINE AND COVENANTS 42:18
Do all murderers become sons of perdition?

Most probably do not. Elder James E. Talmage explained that sons of perdition are only those who "having learned the power of God afterward renounce it; those who sin wilfully in the light of knowledge; those who open their hearts to the Holy Spirit and then put the Lord to a mockery and a shame by denying it" (*Articles of Faith,* 60). Most murderers never meet these qualifications and so cannot become sons of perdition. Perhaps most of them will inherit the telestial kingdom (compare D&C 76:103).

"Restoring what you cannot restore, healing the wound you cannot heal, fixing that which you broke and you cannot fix is the very purpose of the atonement of Christ," taught Elder Boyd K. Packer.

"When your desire is firm and you are willing to pay the 'uttermost farthing' [see Matt. 5:25–26], the law of restitution is suspended. Your obligation is transferred to the Lord. He will settle your accounts.

"I repeat, save for the exception of the very few who defect to perdition, there is no habit, no addiction, no rebellion, no transgression, no apostasy, no crime exempted from the promise of complete forgiveness. That is the promise of the atonement of Christ.

"How all can be repaired, we do not know. It may not all be accomplished in this life" (*Ensign,* Nov. 1995, 19–20; see also D&C 132:26–27).

DOCTRINE AND COVENANTS 42:19
Does the Church believe in capital punishment?

The statement that those who kill shall die may be understood in at least two different senses. First, all who commit sin diminish God's influence in their lives—a condition known as spiritual death. Second, serious offenses, such as murder, may also result in one's life being forfeited. Doctrine and Covenants 42:79 specifies that such punishment is to be meted out only by the law of the land. President Wilford Woodruff wrote: "The revelations of God to this Church make death the penalty for capital crime, and require that offenders against life and property shall be delivered up to and tried by the laws of the land" (*Deseret Weekly,* 12 Dec. 1889).

Elder B. H. Roberts acknowledged "an accusation to the effect that we believe in what is called 'blood atonement.' So, indeed, we do; and so also do the Christian world. Is it not the belief of the Christian world that they will be saved through the atoning blood of Jesus Christ, the Son of God? Most assuredly; and so, too, do we believe in the atonement of the Christ. . . . But the reputation has gone out . . .

that the Church of Jesus Christ of Latter-day Saints, the 'Mormon' Church, arrogates to itself the right to take human life for apostasy from the Church, and for certain other sins. That is a slander; it is not true. We do not believe the doctrine; we do not claim for the Church that it has the right of capital punishment, or the right of executing vengeance" (*Defense of the Faith*, 2:452–53; see also Roberts, *Comprehensive History*, 4:129).

DOCTRINE AND COVENANTS 42:22–26
Why is sexual sin so serious?

Whereas murder tampers with the process by which life ends, sexual sin degrades the process by which life is given.

The First Presidency declared: "The doctrine of this Church is that sexual sin—the illicit sexual relations of men and women stands, in its enormity, next to murder.

"The Lord has drawn no essential distinctions between fornication, adultery, and harlotry or prostitution. Each has fallen under His solemn and awful condemnation." Those who would excuse sexual sin by saying that it "is but a sinless gratification of a normal desire, like appeasing hunger and thirst, speak filthiness with their lips. Their counsel leads to destruction; their wisdom comes from the Father of Lies" (Heber J. Grant, J. Reuben Clark Jr., David O. McKay, in Conference Report, Oct. 1942, 11).

Elder Spencer W. Kimball emphasized that sexual sins "approach the unforgivable ones in seriousness but seem to come in the category of the forgivable. These are the diabolical crimes of sexual impurity. In varied form they run from aberrations involving self-abuse, sex stimulation, and self-pollution to abhorrent and unnatural practices involving others. Whether named or unnamed in scriptures or the spoken word, any sexual act or practice which is 'unnatural' or unauthorized is a sin" (*Miracle of Forgiveness*, 61).

"Sexual immorality is a viper that is striking not only in the world, but in the Church today," concluded President Ezra Taft Benson. "I know the laws of the land do not consider unchastity as serious as God does, nor punish as severely as God does, but that does not change its abominableness. In the eyes of God, chastity will never be out of date" (*Teachings of Ezra Taft Benson*, 279).

DOCTRINE AND COVENANTS 42:30
How can we live the law of consecration today?

Living the law of consecration is still important to us now. Not only was it a key part of the restoration of all things but it was to acquaint us with what will be expected for us to build Zion. Furthermore, the Lord had commanded his people to be one (see D&C 38:27), for, as he explained, "If ye are not equal in earthly things ye cannot be equal in obtaining heavenly things" (D&C 78:6). Living the principles of the law of consecration is a great step toward achieving this unity.

Understanding how this law functioned when it was established in the 1830s can help us appreciate ways in which we can live it today. Recognizing that everything on this earth was truly the Lord's (see Psalm 24:1), the individual consecrated all his property by deed to the bishop, the Lord's authorized temporal representative. The bishop then assigned the consecrator his "stewardship" based not only on the individual or his family's "needs" but also on their "circumstances" (including abilities, talents, and so forth) and on their "just wants" (D&C 51:3; 82:17). Even though the property was regarded as the Lord's, the stewardship over it was given to the individual by formal deed (see D&C 51:4–5). The individual then felt both the usual economic pressures to make a profit and also a spiritual obligation to develop, or magnify, his stewardship to further the Lord's work and to benefit the whole group. The surplus he produced above his family's needs and "just wants" was transferred to the bishop's storehouse. From this source the bishop helped the poor, bought land, erected Church buildings, and took other steps to establish Zion on earth. The surplus could also be used to expand the existing stewardships of all in the order or to improve community living conditions.

Though some of these functions—such as making consecrations or receiving stewardships by formal deed—were suspended in the late 1830s, many principles of the law of consecration still apply today. The concept of stewardship is fostered as we account to priesthood leaders for our service in Church callings. The Church Welfare Program has encouraged members to establish and maintain economic independence, promoted habits of thrift, and created projects through which the Saints work together to help the poor. President J. Reuben Clark Jr. declared: "We have all said that the Welfare Plan is not the United Order and was not intended to be. However, I should like to suggest to you that perhaps, after all, when the Welfare Plan gets thoroughly into operation . . . we shall not be so very far from carrying out the great fundamentals of the United Order" (in Conference Report, Oct. 1942, 57).

In place of the residues and surpluses of the law of consecration, today Church members contribute tithes, fast offerings, and other donations to be used for similar purposes—aiding those in need and building the Church as the kingdom of God on earth. The bishop and his storehouse still play a key role. Elder Marion G. Romney taught: "We as bearers of the priesthood should live strictly by the principles of the United Order, insofar as they are embodied in present church practices, such as the fast offering, tithing, and the welfare activities. Through these practices we could as individuals, if we were of a mind to do so, implement in our own lives all the basic principles of the United Order" (*Improvement Era*, June 1966, 537).

"We must lay on the altar and sacrifice whatever is required by the Lord," counseled President Spencer W. Kimball. "We begin by offering a 'broken heart and a contrite spirit.' We follow this by giving our best effort in our assigned fields of labor and callings. We learn our duty and execute it fully. Finally we consecrate our time, talents, and means, as called upon by our file leaders and as prompted by the whisperings of the Spirit" (in Conference Report, Apr. 1978, 123–24).

DOCTRINE AND COVENANTS 42:43
Is medical help necessary for those with sufficient faith?

Brigham Young chided those who expected to be healed solely by faith without doing anything themselves to help. "If we are sick, and ask the Lord to heal us, and to do all for us that is necessary to be done, according to my understanding of the Gospel of salvation, I might as well ask the Lord to cause my wheat and corn to grow, without my plowing the ground and casting in the seed" (in *Journal of Discourses*, 4:24).

"We must do all we can," affirmed Elder James E. Talmage, "and then ask the Lord to do the rest, such as we cannot do. Hence we hold the medical and surgical profession in high regard. . . . When we have done all we can, then the Divine Power will be directly applicable and operative" (*Church News*, 19 Feb. 1977, 16).

DOCTRINE AND COVENANTS 42:46
Are the faithful promised that they will not die?

The righteous are not promised that they will not die. Reading Doctrine and Covenants 42:46 and 47 carefully shows that they will not "taste of death," meaning that death will hold no fear for them. Death is sweet for the righteous, but it is "bitter" to the disobedient.

DOCTRINE AND COVENANTS 42:48
Does the concept that we may be "appointed unto death" affect our agency?

There is a time appointed when we enter and leave this mortal life. Elder Spencer W. Kimball believed that we may speed up the time of our death through our own careless acts but we probably cannot postpone it very much. He explained: "I believe that many people die before 'their time' because they are careless, abuse their bodies, take unnecessary chances, or expose themselves to hazards, accidents, and sickness. . . .

"God controls our lives, guides and blesses us, but gives us our agency. We may live our lives in accordance with his plan for us or we may foolishly shorten or terminate them" (*Faith Precedes the Miracle*, 103, 105).

"If we are appointed unto death," taught Elder Franklin D. Richards, "we . . . ought to want to go. Our prayers and supplications should be always conditional—that is, if not appointed unto death that he or she should be raised up. And if the heavens want a man to labor there in any sphere, there is where he should be. If a man is wanted to be on a mission in Europe, in Germany, or in the States, and he stays at home, he is not where he ought to be. He ought to be where God would have him, there the Holy Spirit will labor with him and help him. . . . Just so with us. Here we are on a mission in the world. The matter of death is a very small matter. It is a matter of life or death to be sure; but if the Lord does not want us here, and we are taken away, His will be done on earth as it is done in heaven" (in *Journal of Discourses*, 24:285–86).

DOCTRINE AND COVENANTS 42:56–57
What is the status of the Joseph Smith Translation?

President Joseph Fielding Smith wrote: "It has been thought by some, that the Prophet went through the Bible beginning with the first chapter of Genesis and continued through to the Book of Revelation, but this was not the case. He went through the Bible topic by topic, and revising as the Spirit of the Lord indicated to him where changes and additions should be made. There are many parts of the Bible that the Prophet did not touch, because the Lord did not direct him to do so. Therefore, there are many places in the Scriptures where errors still are found. This work was never fully completed, but the Prophet did as much as the Lord commanded him to do before the days of Nauvoo. On February 2, 1833, he finished the revision of the New Testament, and on the second day of July that same year, he finished the Scriptures, as far as the Lord permitted him to go at that time" (*Church History and Modern Revelation*, 1:242; see also Smith, *History of the Church*, 1:324, 368). The Prophet hoped to resume this project in Nauvoo, "but persecution and difficulties prevented him from finishing this work" (Smith and Sjodahl, *Commentary*, 194).

Pursuant to the instructions given in Doctrine and Covenants 42, the Church has not published the entire text of the Joseph Smith Translation, although significant insights have been incorporated into the LDS edition of the King James Version of the Bible. {See D&C 35:20.}

DOCTRINE AND COVENANTS 42:70–73
Why should Church leaders receive support from the Church?

On several occasions the Lord has directed that those who have been called to devote their full time to Church service should be supported by the Church (see D&C 24:3; 41:7; 43:12–13). Doctrine and Covenants 42:70–73 relates this principle of remuneration to the law of consecration. For a few individuals, their full-time Church assignment was their stewardship, the magnifying of which qualified them to receive a living, as was true of other stewardships. The Lord later explained that even though those who administer spiritual things may receive an abundance through the Spirit, they should be equal in temporal things with those whose stewardship is temporal (see D&C 70:12–14).

Thus, Latter-day Saints believe that those who are called to devote their full time to the Church should receive support from the Church. There are at least two major differences between this practice in the restored Church and the "paid ministry" in the churches of the world.

First, the Latter-day Saints cannot choose the ministry as a profession to earn a living because Church callings are made only through those in authority. Second, in contrast to most denominations in which a full-time professional clergy is the rule, among the Latter-day Saints relatively few (such as the General Authorities and mission presidents) are asked to devote all their time to Church work. Instead, most Saints are asked to give part of their time and thus many share in the blessings of Church service.

DOCTRINE AND COVENANTS 42:80–92
What penalties for wrongdoing may the Church impose?

Doctrine and Covenants 42:80–92 distinguishes between the law of the land and religious authority. The procedures to be followed in Church disciplinary councils were outlined more fully in later revelations. {See D&C 102.} A declaration of belief approved in 1835 held that a religious body might take away membership or fellowship but may never deprive any individual of life, liberty, or property (see D&C 134:10).

DOCTRINE AND COVENANTS 43:1–4
Why should a fallen prophet have power to name his successor?

The revelation in Doctrine and Covenants 43 was given at a time when the claims of various individuals professing to receive revelation for the Church caused confusion among the Saints. Specifically, a woman named Hubble announced that she had received by revelation a law for the Church—just as Joseph Smith had done in Doctrine and Covenants 42. To teach the Saints that only the prophet would receive revelations for the Church, the Lord specified that even if the prophet should fall, he would still retain the right to name his successor. Knowing that Joseph Smith would not fall (see D&C 90:3), the Lord was able to make such a startling commitment.

Still, there is a general way in which earlier prophets participate in the selection of their successors. The Lord's great revelation on Church government declared that the Twelve Apostles "form a quorum equal in authority and power" to the First Presidency (D&C 107:24). Thus, when the First Presidency is dissolved by the death of the president, the Twelve become the presiding quorum and their president the presiding officer of the Church. For example, when the First Presidency was organized three years after the death of the Prophet

Joseph Smith on 27 December 1847, the senior apostle and president of the Council of the Twelve, Brigham Young, became the next president of the Church. Since then, whenever the First Presidency has been disorganized by death, the president of the Twelve has succeeded to the presidency of the Church.

The Lord knows who he wants to lead his Church. "The call of one to be President of the Church," instructed President Harold B. Lee, "actually begins when he is called, ordained, and set apart to become a member of the Quorum of the Twelve Apostles. Such a call by prophecy, or in other words, by the inspiration of the Lord to the one holding the keys of presidency, and the subsequent ordination and setting apart by the laying on of hands by that same authority, places each apostle in a priesthood quorum of twelve men holding the apostleship" (in Conference Report, Apr. 1970, 123).

"This is a wise procedure," reflected Elder John A. Widtsoe. "It places at the head of the Church the apostle who has been longest in service. He is known well to the people and trusted by them. He himself knows the procedure of Church affairs. He is no novice to be trained for the position. He can call to his assistance, in addition to his counselors, any helpers from among the priesthood of the Church. It eliminates the shadow of politics from the operations of the Council" (*Evidences and Reconciliations,* 264).

DOCTRINE AND COVENANTS 43:8–9
What is the essential purpose of Church meetings?

We meet together to instruct and build up one another, giving emphasis to understanding and living the gospel. As King Benjamin concluded his great discourse, he challenged his listeners: "And now if you believe all these things see that ye do them" (Mosiah 4:10). Similarly, so that we might profit from what we receive in our meetings, the Lord admonishes us to "bind" ourselves to live according to what we have learned (D&C 43:9).

DOCTRINE AND COVENANTS 43:13
Why were the Saints to provide food and clothing for Joseph Smith?

It is a privilege for the Saints to provide for the temporal needs of those who labor full-time in spiritual matters. {See D&C 42:70–73.}

DOCTRINE AND COVENANTS 43:15–16
Why aren't missionaries to learn from others?

Missionaries do learn many things on their missions, of course, but that is not their purpose for going on a mission. They are commissioned to share with others the precious gospel truths that have been given to us through revelation from God. The broadening that comes to missionaries as they learn a new language or live among people of a different culture is wonderful but not nearly so significant as the spiritual blessings that come to those who teach and to those who are taught (see D&C 18:15–16).

DOCTRINE AND COVENANTS 45:25
What is meant by the phrase "the times of the gentiles"?

First we must understand who the "gentiles" are. President Marion G. Romney taught: "*Gentiles* is the term used by the Book of Mormon prophets to refer to the present inhabitants of America and to the peoples of the old world from which they came" (in Conference Report, Oct. 1975, 54).

The "times of the gentiles" are when these people receive the gospel. In contrast to the meridian of time when the Jews received the gospel first, in the latter days the gentiles were to receive it first and the Jews afterwards (see D&C 90:9; 133:8).

President Joseph Fielding Smith taught: "Jesus said the Jews would be scattered among all nations and Jerusalem would be trodden down by the Gentiles until the times of the Gentiles were fulfilled. (Luke 21:24.) The prophecy in Section 45, verses 24–29, of the Doctrine and Covenants regarding the Jews was literally fulfilled. Jerusalem, which was trodden down by the Gentiles, is no longer trodden down but is made the home for the Jews. They are returning to Palestine, and by this we may know that the times of the Gentiles are near their close" (in Conference Report, Apr. 1966, 13).

DOCTRINE AND COVENANTS 45:32
How can we "stand in holy places"?

The injunction to stand in holy places does not require us to remain in any particular location, but we can make wherever we are a holier place because we live the gospel.

"As one studies the Lord's commandments and attending promises upon compliance therewith," concluded Elder Harold B. Lee, "one gets some definite ideas as to how we might 'stand in holy places,' as the Lord commands. . . . It seems to be made crystal clear that the all-important thing is not where we live but whether or not our hearts are pure" (in Conference Report, Oct. 1968, 62).

DOCTRINE AND COVENANTS 45:39
Why should we want to understand the signs of Christ's coming?

If we are to "prepare for that which is to come" (D&C 1:12), we need to understand what is ahead of us. Perhaps no other scripture gives a more comprehensive outline of the latter days than does Doctrine and Covenants 45. Important details are supplied elsewhere in the standard works (such as in Matthew 24; Joseph Smith–Matthew 1; D&C 29:7–30; 43:17–45; 45; 87; 88:86–116; 101:22–34; 133:1–56) as well as in the teachings of our living prophets.

DOCTRINE AND COVENANTS 45:43
What is "this place" to which the remnant is to gather?

Part of Doctrine and Covenants 45 is a review of the prophecy Christ made to his disciples on the Mount of Olives (compare the latter part of verse 16 with Matthew 24:1–3). Hence, "this place" refers to the Holy Land in the Eastern Hemisphere.

DOCTRINE AND COVENANTS 45:60
To which chapter is the Lord referring?

The Savior's review of his Mount of Olives prophecy concluded with verse 59 of Doctrine and Covenants 45. Hence "this chapter" likely refers to Matthew 24. The manuscript of the Joseph Smith Translation indicates that the Prophet began working on the book of Matthew beginning with chapter 1 the day after Doctrine and Covenants 45 was received in March 1831. He probably completed his work on Matthew 24 before leaving for Missouri in mid-June the same year.

DOCTRINE AND COVENANTS 46:14
Should we be content to base our testimony on the faith of others?

The Savior began his list of spiritual gifts by declaring: "To some it is given by the Holy Ghost to know that Jesus Christ is the Son of God, and that he was crucified for the sins of the world" (D&C 46:13). The position of testimony at the head of the list suggests that personal knowledge or testimony of the Savior is the most fundamental gift for which we should strive. Many, however, have not yet attained this goal of knowing for themselves. Children usually base their faith on the teachings of their parents. New converts often draw strength from the lives of more seasoned Church members. Indeed, we all can and should strengthen one another (see D&C 46:12). The Lord affirmed that "to others it is given to believe on their words, that they also might have eternal life if they continue faithful" (D&C 46:14). One cannot remain at this plateau, however, but must "continue faithful" to the end. "This is a preparatory gift," wrote Truman G. Madsen. "It is not sufficient unto itself. You cannot live and endure and overcome simply on the basis of believing the word of another. Sooner or later, and preferably sooner, you too will come to firsthand and direct knowledge for yourself" (*Joseph Smith the Prophet*, 37).

President Heber C. Kimball warned: "To meet the difficulties that are coming, it will be necessary for you to have a knowledge of the truth of this work for yourselves. . . . If you have not got the testimony, live right and call upon the Lord and cease not till you obtain it. . . .

" . . . The time will come when no man nor woman will be able to endure on borrowed light. Each will have to be guided by the light within himself. If you do not have it, how can you stand?" (quoted by Harold B. Lee, in Conference Report, Oct. 1965, 128).

DOCTRINE AND COVENANTS 46:15–16
What is meant by "differences of administration" and "diversities of operation"?

The phrases "differences of administration" and "diversities of operation" are also found in Paul's list of spiritual gifts (see 1 Corinthians 12:5–6). Understanding what Paul meant by them will help us better understand their significance in the Doctrine and Covenants. Dr. Sidney B. Sperry pointed out that referring to the Greek text of Paul's words clarifies their meaning: "Apparently by 'differences of administration' is meant the distinctive varieties of service and ministration by which things are accomplished in the Church" (*Doctrine and Covenants Compendium*, 196). The 1985 New International Version *Study Bible* notes that "the Greek word in its various forms is used to indicate service to the Christian community" and translates

1 Corinthians 12:5 as follows: "There are different kinds of service, but the same Lord."

Similarly, Dr. Sperry continues, "diversities of operations" refers to "the workings, results, or effects" of various spiritual gifts. "One who by the gift of the Holy Ghost has the gift of knowing the 'diversities of operation' is one who may correctly discern whether a given service is of God or not" (*Doctrine and Covenants Compendium*, 197). The NIV *Study Bible* notes: "The Greek word indicates power that is in operation. Spiritual gifts produce results that are obvious." Its translation of 1 Corinthians 12:6 reads: "There are different kinds of working, but the same God works all of them in all men."

The words of the revelation in Doctrine and Covenants 46 emphasize that the gift is to "know" or understand these things. Priesthood bearers represent the Lord Jesus Christ, and so they should seek his guidance in their service. The Lord has promised that he will direct his servants (see, for example, D&C 100:4–5).

DOCTRINE AND COVENANTS 47:1
What is the value of keeping a history?

The Lord later directed that a history be kept "for the good of the church, and for the rising generations" (D&C 69:8). "The way to [develop faith in the Lord] is to recount the examples of faith that have happened in our history and in our heritage and with our people," declared Elder A. Theodore Tuttle. "That's the value of history." He stated that "we cannot go one generation without losing faith" if we do not keep a faithful history (*Ensign*, Nov. 1986, 73).

Elder Franklin D. Richards expressed appreciation to President Wilford Woodruff who had "from the beginning of his public career kept a journal and a history, and we are indebted in a great measure to his exertion, together with that of some others, for many great and powerful sermons which the Prophet Joseph delivered in the city of Nauvoo. . . . Some of the most important matters pertaining to the most sacred councils that were instituted by the Prophet Joseph are thus brought down to our present time, and by them we are made the happy recipients of many blessings and ordinances" (*Collected Discourses*, 4:272).

Most of us will not be called to keep a Church history, but we have been exhorted to write family or personal histories. These, too, bring blessings. "We may think there is little of interest or importance in what we personally say or do," said President Spencer W. Kimball, "but it is remarkable how many of our families, as we pass on down the line, are interested in all that we do and all that we say. Each of us is important to those who are near and dear to us—and as our posterity read of our life's experiences, they, too, will come to know and love us. And in that glorious day when our families are together in the eternities, we will already be acquainted" (*Ensign*, Nov. 1979, 5).

On another occasion, President Kimball admonished: "If you have not already commenced this important duty in your lives, get a good notebook, a good book that will last through time and into eternity for the angels to look upon. Begin today and write in it your goings and your comings, your deeper thoughts, your achievements, and your failures, your associations and your triumphs, your impressions and your testimonies. We hope you will do this, our brothers and sisters, for this is what the Lord has commanded, and those who keep a personal journal are more likely to keep the Lord in remembrance in their daily lives" (*Ensign*, Dec. 1980, 61).

DOCTRINE AND COVENANTS 49:1–2
What were the results of the mission to the Shakers?

The Shakers, or United Society of Believers in Christ's Second Appearing, had a large community just a few miles southwest of Kirtland. It was to this group that the revelation in section 49 directed the missionaries to go. Ashbel Kitchell, the Shakers' leader, described that when the Latter-day Saint missionaries delivered the message that had been revealed in what we now know as Doctrine and Covenants 49, the Shakers replied that they were satisfied with their own religion.

"On hearing this Rigdon professed to be satisfied, and put his paper by; but Parley Pratt arose and commenced shakeing his coattail; he said he shook the dust from his garments as a testimony against us, that we had rejected the word of the Lord Jesus" (Backman and Cowan, *Joseph Smith and the Doctrine and Covenants*, 55–56).

There is no record that any of these Shakers accepted the restored gospel. Elder Pratt recorded that they "utterly refused to hear or obey the gospel" (*Autobiography of Parley P. Pratt*, 61).

DOCTRINE AND COVENANTS 49:5, 28
Who is speaking here?

Many assume the title "God" always refers to the Father and that

"Lord" refers to the Son. These titles, however, are often used interchangeably. Hence, verse 5 does not clearly identify which one is speaking; verse 28 states that this revelation is from Jesus Christ. This is another example in which the Savior delivers words on behalf of his Father. {See D&C 29:46.}

DOCTRINE AND COVENANTS 49:15–17
What is the place of marriage in God's plan?

The home and family play a central role in our mortal lives. In a historic proclamation Church leaders announced: "We, the First Presidency and the Council of the Twelve Apostles of The Church of Jesus Christ of Latter-day Saints, solemnly proclaim that marriage between a man and a woman is ordained of God and that the family is central to the Creator's plan for the eternal destiny of His children.

"Husband and wife have a solemn responsibility to love and care for each other and for their children. 'Children are an heritage of the Lord' (Psalm 127:3). Parents have a sacred duty to rear their children in love and righteousness, to provide for their physical and spiritual needs, to teach them to love and serve one another, to observe the commandments of God and to be law-abiding citizens wherever they live. Husbands and wives—mothers and fathers—will be held accountable before God for the discharge of these obligations.

"The family is ordained of God. Marriage between man and woman is essential to His eternal plan. Children are entitled to birth within the bonds of matrimony, and to be reared by a father and a mother who honor marital vows with complete fidelity. Happiness in family life is most likely to be achieved when founded upon the teachings of the Lord Jesus Christ" (*Ensign*, Nov. 1995, 101).

LOOKING TOWARD ZION

DOCTRINE AND COVENANTS 52 THROUGH 70

The missionaries to the Lamanites provided the Church with its first contact not only with Ohio but also with Jackson County, Missouri. {See D&C 28:8.} In June 1831, the Lord directed some thirty elders to journey to Missouri where he would identify the land to be consecrated for his people (see D&C 52:2). The Prophet and his associates reached Missouri the following month and learned by revelation where the latter-day Zion would be established (see D&C 57:1–3). The Saints' interest in going to Zion remained keen during the autumn, after Joseph Smith returned to Kirtland. The revelations recorded in Doctrine and Covenants 52 through 70 provide insights on this theme and on a variety of other gospel principles. Near the end of 1831, the year during which most of the revelations in the Doctrine and Covenants were received, steps were underway to publish the first compilation of these revelations (see D&C 67 headnote).

DOCTRINE AND COVENANTS 52:9
What is meant in the instruction to teach
"that which the apostles and prophets have written"?

Although "that which the prophets and apostles have written" refers to the standard works, as Latter-day Saints we give special emphasis to the teachings of our living prophets. Elder Harold B. Lee admonished: "As the Latter-day Saints go home from this [general] conference, it would be well if they consider seriously the importance of taking with them the report of this conference and let it be the guide to their walk and talk during the next six months. These are the important matters the Lord sees fit to reveal to this people in this day" (in Conference Report, Apr. 1946, 68). {See D&C 1:38.}

Also in this verse the Lord again declares the importance of our teaching what we have received through the Holy Ghost. {See D&C 42:12–13.}

DOCTRINE AND COVENANTS 52:10
Why should missionaries go "two by two"?

There are at least two reasons why missionaries go in pairs. First, the scriptures specify that "in the mouth of two or three witnesses shall every word be established" (2 Corinthians 13:1). Missionaries' teaching is most effective when both companions participate, one bearing testimony to what the other has taught. The missionaries' serving in pairs is also a protection not only against physical dangers but also against the devil's temptations.

DOCTRINE AND COVENANTS 52:10
Must confirmations always take place "by the water's side"?

Doctrine and Covenants 52:10 emphasizes that confirmation must follow baptism because the purpose of the laying on of hands is to bestow the gift of the Holy Ghost. Joseph Smith asserted, "You might as well baptize a bag of sand" as to baptize a person without conferring the Holy Ghost. "Baptism by water is but half a baptism, and is good for nothing without the other half—that is, the baptism of the Holy Ghost" (*Teachings of the Prophet Joseph Smith*, 314).

Confirmations are sometimes performed immediately after baptisms, but often they are performed in a sacrament meeting. Because converts are "joining the Church," their being confirmed in the presence of the congregation allows the other Saints to become acquainted with the new members and extend the hand of fellowship to them.

DOCTRINE AND COVENANTS 53:4
What is the role of the agent?

Because the bishop administered the law of consecration, he was responsible for receiving consecrated properties, assigning stewardships, and supervising commodities being transferred in or out of his storehouse. The agent was appointed to assist him in these weighty temporal transactions. When these functions under the law of consecration were suspended, this office was no longer needed. Today, counselors, executive secretaries, and ward clerks assist bishops with their more varied responsibilities.

DOCTRINE AND COVENANTS 54:4–6

What is our accountability when we are prevented from keeping the commandments by the actions of others?

The Lord does not regard us as guilty when we are prevented from keeping his commandments through no fault of our own. He knows our hearts—whether or not we really would willingly have been obedient if given the opportunity. He accepted the efforts of the Saints who had been thwarted in their attempts to build a temple in Missouri, but he gave them an opportunity to demonstrate their good faith by building a temple in Nauvoo (see D&C 124:49–55).

DOCTRINE AND COVENANTS 56:4

If God is unchanging, why would he ever revoke his commandments?

Even though God does not change, our circumstances do. His purposes and gospel principles are unchanging, but the means of carrying out those purposes and principles may vary from one circumstance to another. For example, the principle of taking care of our physical bodies is unchanging, but specific dietary laws essential in ancient Israel are not necessary now and are not applicable today.

That the Lord made the seemingly routine matter of the reassignment of missionary companions a subject of revelation should remind us to keep ourselves receptive to his guidance even in what we may regard as the ordinary aspects of our lives.

DOCTRINE AND COVENANTS 56:16–18

Is worldly wealth, as such, good or evil?

Money can be an instrument either for good or for evil. It is needed to construct temples and to support the Lord's work in many other ways. For example, we have been commanded to contribute funds to benefit the poor (see D&C 42:30) and to support the programs of the Church (see D&C 119:2). Nevertheless, when we make the acquisition of riches an end in itself, our life is diverted from following more important spiritual values. {See D&C 6:7.} Paul declared that "the love of money [rather than money itself] is the root of all evil" (1 Timothy 6:10; compare Matthew 19:16–24). In Doctrine and Covenants 56:16–18 the Lord made the same point—it is not the presence or the absence of wealth but rather our attitudes that may be good or bad.

DOCTRINE AND COVENANTS 58:41
Shouldn't we seek to excel?

We should always strive to do our best, but our reasons for doing so must be considered. On one occasion, for example, the Prophet Joseph Smith admonished: "Let the Twelve be humble, and not be exalted, and beware of pride, and not seek to excel one above another" (*History of the Church,* 3:383). In another instance, Sidney Rigdon was directed to write a description of the land of Zion together with a statement of God's purposes concerning it (see D&C 58:50). Unfortunately, Sidney "exalted himself in his heart," and the Lord did not approve his document (D&C 63:55–56). Apparently William W. Phelps suffered from a similar problem because he not only sought "to excel" but also was "not sufficiently meek" (D&C 58:41).

DOCTRINE AND COVENANTS 58:43
To whom should we confess our sins?

We are to confess all our shortcomings to our Heavenly Father through prayer. The more specific we can be, even in our private prayers, the more completely we can bring ourselves to recognize and acknowledge areas in which we need to repent. Alma described the peace we feel when we have obtained our Father's forgiveness (see Alma 36:17–21).

We should also confess our sins to those whom we have hurt or offended and humbly ask their forgiveness. In an earlier revelation (see D&C 42:88–92) the Lord instructed that only those affected by our transgressions need to be involved in our process of repentance. "Keep your follies that do not concern others to yourselves," cautioned President Brigham Young (*Discourses of Brigham Young,* 158).

Although we may acknowledge our weaknesses and shortcomings in a general way to our fellow Saints and ask their help in overcoming them, we have been counseled not to detail our sins inappropriately in public. Elder Theodore M. Burton observed: "Confessions to others— particularly confessions repeated in open meetings, unless the sin has been a public sin requiring public forgiveness—only demean both the confessor and the hearer" (*Ensign,* Aug. 1988, 9).

We should confess to Church leaders when our sins are such that our standing in the Church might be in question. {See D&C 102.} There may be other circumstances in which we might discuss our problems with a bishop or branch president to enlist his help. In no case do our leaders forgive on behalf of the Lord—he does that for himself; they can, however, extend forgiveness on behalf of the Church as an organization.

DOCTRINE AND COVENANTS 59:9–12
How can we know which activities are appropriate for the Sabbath?

Rather than thinking of things we should not do on Sunday, we might more profitably consider the purposes of this holy day. Doctrine and Covenants 59 emphasizes two of them:

First, we should worship God, carry out our religious responsibilities, and promote our spiritual growth. "If we are not present at our meetings when we have the opportunity," said President Anthon H. Lund, "we deprive ourselves of great blessings; in fact, we will be starving spiritually. At our meetings we receive instruction, encouragement to do right, and we enjoy the influence of the Spirit of God" (in Conference Report, Oct. 1916, 10). President Spencer W. Kimball taught: "We may want to set aside time for our family to be together, for personal study and meditation, and for service to others. We might want to read the scriptures, conference reports, and Church publications; study the lives and teachings of the prophets; prepare church lessons and other church assignments; write in journals; pray and meditate; write to or visit relatives and friends; write to missionaries; enjoy uplifting music; have family gospel instruction; hold family council meetings; build husband-wife relationships; read with a child; do genealogical research, including the four-generation program and family or personal histories; sing Church hymns; read uplifting literature; develop our appreciation of the cultural arts; plan family home evening study and activities; plan other family activities; friendship nonmembers; fellowship neighbors; visit the sick, the aged, and the lonely; hold interviews with family members" (*Ensign*, Jan. 1982, 3).

Second, we should rest from our daily work. The Sabbath provides a break from our labors that may actually make us more productive in the long run.

On Sunday we avoid certain activities that are appropriate on other days, not because they are wrong but because we want a different emphasis on the Sabbath. The Lord taught that typical Sunday activities are also appropriate on other days (see D&C 59:11). Though there may be a shift in emphasis on the Lord's day, our lives should be such that there is not an abrupt break between the Sabbath and the rest of the week.

DOCTRINE AND COVENANTS 59:12
What are the "oblations" we should offer?

A dictionary published in Joseph Smith's day defined *oblation* as "any thing offered or presented in worship or sacred service; an offering; a sacrifice" (Webster, *American Dictionary*). Not just tithes or other monetary offerings but all our appropriate Sabbath activities might well be regarded as "oblations."

DOCTRINE AND COVENANTS 59:13–14
Why should "fasting" be equated with "rejoicing"?

Fasting should be a positive rather than a negative experience. By going without physical food, we remind ourselves that our spirit is ultimately more important. During our fast we should engage in activities that nourish the spirit—prayer, searching the scriptures, serving others, and so forth. The Savior has promised that as we turn our attention to him, he will impart the Spirit, which not only enlightens our minds but also fills our souls with joy (see D&C 11:13). Hence fasting truly is intertwined with joy and rejoicing.

DOCTRINE AND COVENANTS 61
Should we always stay away from water?

After reading this revelation only casually, some have reached the erroneous conclusion that we should avoid water. Yet water is used in the ordinances of baptism and the sacrament, in which it represents a cleansing, specifically through the atoning blood of Jesus Christ.

The revelation in Doctrine and Covenants 61 warned the brethren against physical dangers on the waters and also reminded them that Satan had power over the waters (see vv. 4–5, 19). Nevertheless, the faithful are promised that they will be protected and that the Spirit will guide them (see v. 6). "Notwithstanding the great power of Satan upon the waters," testified President Joseph Fielding Smith, "the Lord still held command, and he could protect his people whether on land or by water as they journeyed" (*Church History and Modern Revelation*, 1:225).

Elder LeGrand Richards related an example of such protection.

Over the years, "it was considered as good as an insurance policy when a company of Latter-day Saints embarked on a vessel crossing the Atlantic. I recall reading in my grandfather's diary of a time when the boat upon which he was sailing was in great jeopardy, so much so that the captain of the boat came to him and pleaded with him to intercede with the Lord in behalf of the boat and her passengers; and Grandfather, remembering that he had been promised that he should have power over the elements, walked out on the deck of the boat and raised his hands to high heaven and rebuked the sea and the waves, and they were immediately calmed, and the appreciation of the captain of the boat was so great that he offered him the use of his private quarters during the balance of the journey" (in Conference Report, Apr. 1941, 84).

The Lord teaches us an important principle in this revelation. "It mattereth not" whether his servants travel by water or by land, "if it so be that they fill their mission" (v. 22). He admonishes all of us to be guided by the Spirit so that we might know what to do in any situation (see vv. 27–28).

DOCTRINE AND COVENANTS 63:7–10
Why can't faith be based on signs? What about instances where people asked for miraculous proofs and received them?

The "signs" spoken of in Doctrine and Covenants 63 are external proofs. Because signs come through faith, the Master condemned those who demanded such proofs as a substitute for faith or for personal gratification (see Matthew 12:38–39). Nevertheless, on occasion the Lord has employed miraculous manifestations to bring about the conversion of individuals who would play key roles in his work. Examples include the apostle Paul (see Acts 9:1–18; 22:3–13) and Alma the Younger and the four sons of King Mosiah (see Mosiah 27:8–36; Alma 36:6–24). In a few instances the Lord has consented to help an individual whose faith was weak but whose potential was great; Gideon is one of these (see Judges 6:36–40). Korihor is clearly an example of the wicked who demanded a sign and received one—"but not unto salvation" (D&C 63:7; see also Alma 30:48–56).

We perceive signs through our human senses and judge their validity with human reason, yet our senses can be deceived, and our reason is fallible. Faith based on such an uncertain foundation cannot be secure. The scriptures and sacred history are full of examples of individuals who fell away after basing their faith on signs (see, for example, 1 Nephi 3:29–31).

The scriptures promise that "signs shall follow them that believe" (Mark 16:17). The purpose of these signs is to bless individuals and give miraculous help in spreading the Lord's work. With the gift of discernment, the faithful can know the divine source of such miracles. But the greatest of such signs is the witness through the Spirit. Unlike external wonders that must be experienced by our imperfect senses, the Spirit communicates his witness directly to our spirit, bypassing our human uncertainties.

DOCTRINE AND COVENANTS 63:17
What are the "lake which burneth with fire" and the "second death"?

The "second death" is a spiritual death suffered permanently only by the sons of perdition (see D&C 29:41). When we sin, we bring a condition of spiritual death upon ourselves as we are estranged from God, who is the source of our spiritual life. Through the atonement of Christ, this estrangement will be overcome, at least temporarily, when we are brought back into God's presence to be judged. Those few who have become sons of perdition will then suffer a second spiritual death when they are cut off, this time permanently, from all contact with God's glory and influence (see Helaman 14:15–18).

The "lake of fire" is an allusion to Gehenna, a dreadful, sulfurous place just outside Jerusalem where rotting garbage was constantly being burned. Ancient prophets chose this place as a fitting representation of eternal torment. The Book of Mormon clarifies that references to the lake of fire and brimstone are only symbolic (see 2 Nephi 9:16; Alma 12:17). King Benjamin taught that the torment of the damned is actually the anguish of guilt (see Mosiah 2:38; 3:25–27).

Those who will ultimately inherit the telestial kingdom experience this torment as a temporary condition in the spirit prison (compare D&C 63:17 with 76:103–9). This torment, however, will be the eternal fate of those who become sons of perdition (see D&C 76:30–37). {See D&C 76:84.}

DOCTRINE AND COVENANTS 63:20–21
When will the earth be transfigured?

Our earth has already passed through two major changes. First, at the time of Adam's fall, the earth itself—which originally was in a celestial condition, having been created spiritually in heaven (see Moses 3:5)—fell into a paradisiacal, or terrestrial, state. At the time of the Fall, the earth came into its present telestial condition.

Two more changes are future, and either of them might be the "transfiguration" spoken of in Doctrine and Covenants 63:20–21. Third, at the time of Christ's second coming, the "earth will be renewed and receive [once again] its paradisiacal glory" (Article of Faith 10). It will be cleansed by fire, the wicked being burned as stubble (see Malachi 4:1). During the thousand years of the Millennium the earth will again be in a terrestrial condition. Fourth, after the thousand years are ended, the earth will be completely consumed by fire. The old earth will pass away, and there will be a new heaven and a new earth (see 3 Nephi 26:3; Revelation 21:1). President Joseph Fielding Smith noted that like its inhabitants, the earth too shall die, pass through the resurrection, and be raised to an immortal, unchangeable condition as the eternal abode for such inhabitants as the Lord in his wisdom will place upon it (see *Restoration of All Things*, 293–97).

In its final celestial condition, the earth may be described as a "sea of glass," or a giant Urim and Thummim (see D&C 77:1; 130:8–9; see also D&C 137:2–4). Surely the faithful will have an inheritance as promised in Doctrine and Covenants 63:20–21, both during the Millennium and on the glorious celestialized earth.

DOCTRINE AND COVENANTS 63:23
What are the "mysteries of the kingdom"?

Because a mystery is something we cannot know through human resources alone, it must be made known by revelation. {See D&C 6:7.} In Doctrine and Covenants 63:23 the Lord sets forth the truth that such revelations can come only to the obedient. He also suggests what kind of mysteries will be revealed—truths that will help us in our quest for exaltation, or eternal life.

DOCTRINE AND COVENANTS 63:34
What is meant by the promise that the Saints will "hardly escape"?

Hardly meant "scarcely; barely; almost not," referring to something achieved only "with difficulty; with great labor" (Webster, *American Dictionary*). The Lord has promised that Zion and her stakes will be places of defense and refuge when the divine wrath will be "poured out without mixture upon the whole earth" (D&C 115:6). Still the faithful will not be totally shielded from these difficulties, and great effort will be required to maintain the righteous conditions that will spare them (see D&C 97:25–26).

DOCTRINE AND COVENANTS 64:9–10
Why will God forgive only certain people whereas we must forgive everybody?

The statement "I, the Lord, will forgive whom I will" may seem arbitrary, but the scriptures repeatedly state that God will forgive those who repent (see D&C 1:31–33; 58:42–43, for example). Because of our imperfections, we cannot always know for sure who has repented; hence, we should always forgive without trying to judge. {See D&C 98:23–48.} Furthermore, this commandment was given to a people who, like us, were looking forward to establishing Zion. The willingness to forgive always is essential to the unity required for building Zion (see Moses 7:18; D&C 38:27).

DOCTRINE AND COVENANTS 64:21
How long did the Lord's "strong hold" actually survive in Kirtland?

The weeks preceding the dedication of the Kirtland Temple in March 1836 were the peak of growth and development in Kirtland. In fact, this was one of the greatest spiritual seasons known in Church history. During the fall of that same year, however, the first signs of dissension and faithlessness appeared and soon grew into full-blown apostasy. Thus the Lord's "strong hold in the land of Kirtland" lasted almost exactly the five years he had decreed.

DOCTRINE AND COVENANTS 64:23
What is the connection between paying tithing and not being burned?

On several occasions the Lord has made the connection between paying tithing and escaping the burning of the wicked (see Malachi 3:8–10; 4:1; D&C 85:3). Surely a wicked person cannot hope to escape the consequences of his general disobedience merely by honoring one commandment. Some attend church because of social motivations, others keep the Word of Wisdom to secure better health, and yet these outwardly righteous acts do not necessarily indicate general faithfulness. Tithe paying, on the other hand, is a very personal matter—more likely to be done for the right reasons. Therefore one who pays his tithing is apt to keep God's other commandments as well, earning the promised protection from prophesied latter-day burnings and judgments.

President Joseph F. Smith affirmed that through obedience to the law of tithing, "the loyalty of the people of this Church shall be put to the test. By this principle it shall be known who is for the kingdom of God and who is against it. By this principle it shall be seen whose hearts are set on doing the will of God and keeping his commandments" (*Gospel Doctrine*, 225).

"The man who does not learn how to give can never attain spiritual greatness," asserted Elder John A. Widtsoe. "A person who is so wedded to temporal things that he cannot part with some of them is not a fit candidate for any kingdom of God" (*Message of the Doctrine and Covenants*, 97).

On the positive side, Elder Howard W. Hunter testified: "The payment of tithing strengthens faith, increases spirituality and spiritual capacity, and solidifies testimony. It gives the satisfaction of knowing one is complying with the will of the Lord. It brings the blessings that come from sharing with others through the purposes for which tithing is used. We cannot afford to deny ourselves these blessings. We cannot afford not to pay our tithing" (in Conference Report, Apr. 1964, 36).

DOCTRINE AND COVENANTS 65:2–6
What is the "kingdom of God"?

The phrase "kingdom of God" has been used in at least two different senses. "The kingdom of God is a preparation for the kingdom of heaven, which is yet to come," explained Elder James E. Talmage. "The expressions 'Kingdom of God' and 'Kingdom of Heaven' are ofttimes used synonymously and interchangeably." But "the light of modern revelation" clarifies "that there is a distinction between the kingdom of God and the kingdom of heaven. The kingdom of God is the Church of Christ; the kingdom of heaven is that system of government and administration which is operative in heaven, and which we pray may some day prevail on earth" (in Conference Report, Apr. 1917, 65).

Speaking of that millennial state, President Joseph Fielding Smith taught: "This government which embraces all the peoples of the earth, both in and out of the Church, is also sometimes spoken of as the kingdom of God, because the people are subject to the kingdom of God which Christ will set up; but they have their agency and thousands will not be members of the Church until they are converted; yet at the same time they will be subject to the theocratic rule.

"When our Savior comes to rule in the millennium, all governments will become subject unto his government" (*Doctrines of Salvation,* 1:229).

Elder LeGrand Richards viewed the establishment of the Savior's kingdom as one of the most significant fulfillments of prophecies concerning the last days: "If the inhabitants of this earth had the ability and the power to read the signs of the times, they would know that already the Lord has given far more than the darkening of the sun or obscuring the light of the moon or causing the stars to fall from heaven, for what he has accomplished in the establishment of his kingdom in the earth in these latter days, and the unseen power operating in the world for the accomplishment of his purposes, are greater signs than any of these phenomena that we read about—the signs of his coming" (in Conference Report, Apr. 1951, 41).

"The Church will not be taken from the earth again," testified President Ezra Taft Benson. "It is here to stay. The Lord has promised it and you are a part of that Church and kingdom—the nucleus around which will be builded the great kingdom of God on the earth. The kingdom of heaven and the kingdom of God on the earth will be combined together at Christ's coming—and that time is not far distant. How I wish we could get the vision of this work, the genius of it, and realize the nearness of that great event. I am sure it would have a sobering effect upon us if we realized what is before us" (*Teachings of Ezra Taft Benson,* 19).

DOCTRINE AND COVENANTS 65:2–6
To what extent has the kingdom of God "filled the whole earth"?

In 1900, after the Church had been in existence for seventy years, it had just over a quarter of a million members. Estimates of Church membership by the end of the twentieth century are about 11.3 million, but at the same time there will be an estimated world population of about 6.7 billion—in other words, more than 500 other people for each Latter-day Saint.

Nevertheless, the Church's membership is becoming more widely distributed geographically. At midcentury more than nine of ten Latter-day Saints lived in the United States and Canada; by the end of the century they will represent less than half the membership of the Church.

DOCTRINE AND COVENANTS 67:4–8
Was this challenge to duplicate a revelation accepted? What happened?

Doubts were raised at the conference that was considering publishing the collected revelations when certain brethren criticized Joseph Smith's language. Such criticisms should not have been taken seriously, because in a revelation received during that same conference the Lord had explained that these revelations "were given unto my servants in their weakness, after the manner of their language, that they might come to understanding" (D&C 1:24). Still, the Lord challenged the critics to "appoint him that is the most wise among you" and have him try to duplicate the "least" of the revelations given through the Prophet (D&C 67:6).

Joseph Smith recorded that in response to this challenge, William E. McLellin "as the wisest man, in his own estimation, having more learning than sense, endeavored to write a commandment like unto one of the least of the Lord's, but failed; it was an awful responsibility to write in the name of the Lord" (*History of the Church*, 1:226). The Lord fulfilled his promise that a "stupor of thought" would result from that which was wrong (see D&C 9:9).

DOCTRINE AND COVENANTS 67:10
Can we really behold God's face in this life?

A few statements in the Bible have led people to believe that it is impossible to behold God's face. One of these is Exodus 33:20; nevertheless, only nine verses earlier, we read that "the Lord spake unto Moses face to face, as a man speaketh unto his friend" (Exodus 33:11). What then do these biblical passages mean?

Joseph Smith's inspired "translation" provides the following clarifications:

"And no man hath seen God at any time, except he hath borne record of the Son" (JST, John 1:19).

"No man hath seen God at any time, except them who believe" (1 John 4:12). {See **D&C 35:20**.}

Other latter-day revelation adds further insight: "For no man has seen God at any time in the flesh, except quickened by the Spirit of God" (D&C 67:11; compare Moses 1:11).

The promise in Doctrine and Covenants 67:10 that we can see God was repeated on other occasions (see D&C 93:1; 97:15–17; 110:7–8). The Prophet Joseph Smith taught: "After a person has faith in Christ, repents of his sins, and is baptized for the remission of his sins and receives the Holy Ghost, (by the laying on of hands), which is the first Comforter, then let him continue to humble himself before God, hungering and thirsting after righteousness, and living by every word of God, and the Lord will soon say unto him, Son thou shalt be exalted. When the Lord has thoroughly proved him, and finds that the man is determined to serve Him at all hazards, then the man will find his calling and his election made sure, then it will be his privilege to receive the other Comforter.

"When any man obtains this last Comforter, he will have the personage of Jesus Christ to attend him, or appear unto him from time to time, and even He will manifest the Father unto him" (*Teachings of the Prophet Joseph Smith,* 150–51).

We must pay a high price to be worthy to have this exalted experience. Although it may not come in this life, we should nevertheless strive to be worthy of receiving this blessing whenever the Savior should choose to extend it to us.

On special occasions Church leaders have testified that they have enjoyed the fulfillment of this promise. "I know that God lives," affirmed President George Q. Cannon. "I know that Jesus lives; for I have seen Him" (*Deseret Weekly,* 6 Oct. 1896).

Elder Melvin J. Ballard bore a similar witness: "I know, as well as I know that I live and look into your faces, that Jesus Christ lives. . . . For in the visions of the Lord to my soul, I have seen Christ's face, I have heard his voice. I know that he lives" (in Conference Report, Apr. 1920, 40).

DOCTRINE AND COVENANTS 67:10–12
What is meant by "natural" and "carnal"?

Doctrine and Covenants 67:10 contrasts what is "carnal" and "natural" with that which is "spiritual." Other scriptures use these words in a similar sense (see, for example, Romans 8:6 and 1 Corinthians 2:14). *Carnal* literally means "pertaining to the flesh." We can sense the meaning of *natural* as we see how King Benjamin contrasted the "natural man" with one who "yields to the enticings of the Holy Spirit and putteth off the natural man and becometh a saint" (Mosiah 3:19). Thus, in the scriptures, *carnal* and *natural* mean "sinful, unspiritual, or worldly."

"We may see God by the quickened spirit," explained Elder John A. Widtsoe. "No man who lives merely in a carnal world can ever know God. There is power in man to lift himself out of the material world into the spiritual realm. So declares this revelation. It emphasizes that 'The flesh may be quickened.' It does not necessarily mean that we can see God with these mortal eyes. We do not fully know the procedure, but whatever it means it cannot be realized except as man rises out of his carnal manner of living" (*Message of the Doctrine and Covenants*, 47).

DOCTRINE AND COVENANTS 68:16–18
Why do literal descendants of Aaron have a special right to the office of bishop?

In Old Testament times the descendants of Aaron were the priests; the firstborn or eldest among them presided as high priest. Today the responsibility of presiding over the lesser priesthood has been assigned to the bishop (see D&C 107:88).

President Joseph Fielding Smith explained: "As the office of bishop belongs to the Aaronic Priesthood, and since that Priesthood was conferred upon Aaron and his posterity after him, the descendants of Aaron have a legal right to this Priesthood. . . . The office of Presiding Bishop of the Church is the same as the office which was held by Aaron." President Smith continued, "It is the highest office, holding the presidency in the Aaronic Priesthood. . . . should it be shown by revelation that there is one who is the 'firstborn among the sons of Aaron,' and thus entitled by birthright to this presidency, he could 'claim' his 'anointing' and the right to that office in the Church" (*Church History and Modern Revelation*, 1:259).

DOCTRINE AND COVENANTS 68:27
Why is eight years an appropriate age of accountability?

Individuals develop step by step. The Lord declared that as children grow, they "begin to become accountable before me" (D&C 29:47). Research has demonstrated that "between the ages of 6 and 11, . . . children become less dependent on their parents and more responsible for making their own decisions and governing their own behavior" (Berger and Thompson, *Developing Person*, 389). Specifically, between the ages of seven and eight, they "begin to understand the basic principles that underlie their behavior" (*Compton's Encyclopedia*, 4:327).

DOCTRINE AND COVENANTS 70:6–13
Why was Joseph Smith to benefit from the sale of the published revelations?

Those like Joseph Smith who have been assigned a spiritual stewardship are to have support just as did those with the usual temporal stewardships. The Church therefore had a responsibility to provide for the Prophet and his family. {See D&C 42:70–73.} This revelation suggested a source for the funds needed to discharge that obligation.

TRANSLATING THE SCRIPTURES

DOCTRINE AND COVENANTS 71 THROUGH 76

During the winter of 1831–32, Joseph Smith continued his translation of the Bible. {See **D&C 35:20.**} This demanding task stimulated questions about the meaning of biblical passages. These questions resulted in revelations that, among other things, shed light on Paul's teachings about marriage (see D&C 74) and on the three degrees of glory (see D&C 76).

The Prophet's translating was interrupted when he was directed to respond to some early attacks against the Church (see D&C 71). Important organizational developments during this time included the calling of a second bishop (see D&C 72) and Joseph Smith's being sustained as president of the high priesthood (see D&C 75 headnote).

DOCTRINE AND COVENANTS 71:1
Why should missionaries expound the mysteries?

A superficial reading of this directive may give the impression that the brethren were to delve into topics on which the Lord has not spoken. That could not be further from the truth. The context clarifies that the missionaries are to proclaim fundamental concepts that had been revealed—"my gospel, the things of the kingdom . . . out of the scriptures." {See **D&C 6:7.**}

DOCTRINE AND COVENANTS 72:16–19
How does the Church presently recommend members when they move?

When a Church member moves from one location to another, his official record of membership is transferred from one ward or branch to another. The original method of making such transfers has been superseded by modern technology, but the purpose is still the same—to document one's standing in the Church. {See **D&C 20:81–84.**} Church leaders in the area where the member is moving are instructed to extend callings only after receiving the individual's records. These records in the past were often called "membership recommends."

DOCTRINE AND COVENANTS 73:3
What was Joseph Smith to "translate" at this time?

The Prophet was to resume work on his inspired revision, or translation of the Bible. {See D&C 35:20.} Several sections in the Doctrine and Covenants are revelations received in response to questions Joseph had about biblical passages. These include sections 74, 76, 77, 91, and 113.

DOCTRINE AND COVENANTS 74
What did Paul teach about interfaith marriages?

The apostle Paul pointed out in 1 Corinthians 7:12–14 how a faithful Church member could, through his or her influence and example, convert a nonmember spouse and bring the sanctifying blessings of the gospel into their family. They would thereby save not only themselves but also their children from being subject to false traditions. Paul did not advocate marrying an unbeliever, however; to the contrary, he recognized the inadvisability of being "unequally yoked together with unbelievers" (2 Corinthians 6:14).

After quoting 1 Corinthians 7:14 (see D&C 74:1), the Lord pointed out a pitfall in interfaith marriages: an "unbelieving" or non-Christian father, for example, could influence his children to follow the old Mosaic law rather than the gospel of Christ and thus deprive his family of the sanctifying blessings the gospel brings.

DOCTRINE AND COVENANTS 75:20–21
Why should one be "filled with joy and gladness" despite knowing that others must be condemned?

The ceremony of shaking dust off the feet symbolized missionaries' having discharged their duty to teach and warn. {See D&C 24:15.} Knowing that we have fulfilled our duty should always be a source of satisfaction. The missionaries were to be "filled with joy" not because those who had rejected them would be condemned but because they themselves had faithfully done their duty.

DOCTRINE AND COVENANTS 76:17
What is the significance of Joseph Smith's inspired revisions of John 5:29?

The Prophet's changes may not seem very significant when comparing Doctrine and Covenants 76:17 with John 5.29. They are, however, much more important than they may appear at first glance.

Many in Joseph's day believed that there were only two conditions in eternity: heaven and hell. The wording in the King James Version of John 5:29 seems to support the doctrine that all will be resurrected "unto" either "life" or "damnation." Yet having only these two conditions does not allow for the wide variety that exists among the earth's inhabitants. The Prophet's revision in Doctrine and Covenants 76 shifts the emphasis from two ultimate states to two major divisions in the resurrection itself: individuals will come forth in the "resurrection of the just" or of the "unjust." The remainder of this revelation explains that there will be four kingdoms with a variety of rewards based on how each person has lived his or her life.

DOCTRINE AND COVENANTS 76:22–23
What is meant by the phrase "last of all"?

On the Brigham Young University campus certain guest speakers have been invited to deliver their "last lecture," setting forth what they would want to emphasize in the last message they ever gave. Perhaps that is the spirit in which the phrase "last of all" is used here. What was this significant "last" witness? "That he [Christ] lives!"

Over the centuries philosophers have debated the merits of various arguments for the existence of God. Alma is one of many who have advanced reasons for their faith in God (see Alma 30:44). Such skeptics as Korihor have rejected these arguments, claiming it is impossible to know there is a God (see Alma 30:13, 15, 28). Ultimately each of us can answer this crucial question only for ourselves, according to our own spiritual witness. Note the directness of the evidence Joseph Smith and Sidney Rigdon gave for their testimony of God's existence: they had seen him (see D&C 76:23).

DOCTRINE AND COVENANTS 76:24

What do we know about the other worlds Christ created?
How does the Atonement performed on this earth relate to them?

The prophet Moses learned that Christ was instrumental in creating "worlds without number" (Moses 1:33). Joseph Smith, in a poetic paraphrase of Doctrine and Covenants 76, wrote that Jesus Christ was not only the Creator but also the Savior of these worlds:

> And I heard a great voice bearing record from heav'n,
> He's the Saviour, and only begotten of God—
> By him, of him, and through him, the worlds were all made,
> Even all that career in the heavens so broad,
> Whose inhabitants, too, from the first to the last,
> Are sav'd by the very same Saviour of ours;
> And, of course, are begotten God's daughters and sons,
> By the very same truths, and the very same pow'rs.
> (*Times and Seasons,* 1 Feb. 1843, 82–83)

By means of a parable about a "lord of the field" visiting various servants in succession, the Master taught that he would visit and bless the inhabitants of the several kingdoms he had created (see D&C 88:51–61). Concerning the universality of the Savior's work, Elder Marion G. Romney declared, "Except for his mortal ministry accomplished on this earth, his service and relationship to other worlds and their inhabitants are the same as his service and relationship to this earth and its inhabitants" (*Improvement Era,* Nov. 1968, 46).

DOCTRINE AND COVENANTS 76:25–28

What do the adversary's various titles tell us about him?

Two of Satan's names in these verses refer to his high standing in the premortal councils. The name *Lucifer* is derived from the Latin *lux* (meaning "light") combined with the Latin *ferre* (meaning "to bring, carry, or bear"); hence this name literally means "light bearer." He was "a son of the morning," suggesting his preeminence as one of God's first spirit children to be born and as one "in authority in the presence of God."

The other titles describe his condition after his rebellion and fall. *Devil* comes from the Greek *diabolos,* meaning "slanderer," perhaps recalling his wanting to take God's honor. The name *Satan* comes from the Hebrew *Saatan,* meaning "an enemy or one who plots against."

Perdition is derived from the Latin verb *perdere* (meaning "to lose") so *perdition* literally means "loss." Satan and those who follow him lose the privilege of being in any of the kingdoms of glory.

Our appreciation for the Adversary's powers of persuasion must be enhanced when we remember that he was able in God's very presence to draw away one-third of the spirits after him. He still possesses these powers today.

DOCTRINE AND COVENANTS 76:31-35
What are the actions a person takes to become a son of perdition, and what does it mean to deny the Holy Ghost?

A person who becomes a son of perdition must know the gospel is true and have experienced God's power and then deliberately and knowingly deny that certain knowledge (see Alma 39:6). Joseph Smith said it is like a person claiming that "the sun does not shine while he sees it" (*Teachings of the Prophet Joseph Smith*, 358). The Lord declared that one not only "denies" what he knows to be true but must also "defy" God's power (D&C 76:31). To defy God's power involves a willful opposition to him and his work. The Savior likens this unpardonable offense to knowingly participating in his crucifixion and exposing him "to an open shame" (D&C 76:35).

Some have wondered why we can be forgiven after blaspheming Christ but not for denying the Holy Ghost (see Matthew 12:31–32; Luke 12:10). The difference seems to be not the object of one's blasphemy but rather whether it involves repudiating the certain witness that comes from the Holy Ghost. "The testimony of the Spirit," affirmed President Joseph Fielding Smith, "is so great, and the impressions and revelations of divine truth so forcefully revealed that there comes to the recipient a conviction of the truth that he cannot forget. Therefore, when a person once enlightened by the Spirit so that he receives knowledge that Jesus Christ is the Only Begotten Son of God in the flesh, then turns away and fights the Lord and his work, he does so against the light and testimony he has received by the power of God. Therefore, he has resigned himself to evil knowingly. Therefore Jesus said there is no forgiveness for such a person.

"The testimony of the Holy Ghost is the strongest testimony that a man can receive" (*Answers to Gospel Questions*, 4:92). The Lord explained that the sons of perdition are those who "deny the Son after the Father has revealed him" through the Holy Ghost (D&C 76:43).

DOCTRINE AND COVENANTS 76:36-39
What will be the state of the sons of perdition?

The Lord described the fate of the sons of perdition as a "lake of fire and brimstone" and called it a "second death." {See D&C 63:17.} The sons of perdition will be resurrected (see D&C 76:39 n. a), but they cannot be redeemed from the effects of their sins because they do not repent. Even though the Lord has not revealed the full extent of their torment (see D&C 76:45-46), what he has told us should be sufficient to warn us away from this fate.

DOCTRINE AND COVENANTS 76:48
Who are "ordained" unto condemnation?

The idea that God has predestined some of his children to damnation is false. He has, however, "ordained" or decreed laws. Keeping them brings blessings (see D&C 130:20-21) and breaking them inevitably brings penalties, including condemnation (see Alma 42:22). The Savior has thus ordained a system in which we ourselves determine whether or not we must be condemned.

DOCTRINE AND COVENANTS 76:53
What does it mean to be "sealed by the Holy Spirit of promise"?

The title "Holy Spirit of promise" refers to the "sealing and ratifying power of the Holy Ghost," taught Elder Bruce R. McConkie, "that is, the power given him to ratify and approve the righteous acts of men so that those acts will be binding on earth and in heaven" (*Mormon Doctrine*, 361). He places a stamp of approval on ordinances we receive worthily or when we become worthy of them later on.

The ultimate promise, which follows a faithful couple's sealing in the temple, is of eternal life in the celestial kingdom (see D&C 88:3-4). We can lie our way into the temple and receive sacred ordinances there, said Elder Melvin J. Ballard. "We may deceive men but we cannot deceive the Holy Ghost, and our blessings will not be eternal unless they are also sealed by the Holy Spirit of Promise, the Holy Ghost, one who reads the thoughts and hearts of men and gives his sealing approval to the blessings pronounced upon their heads. Then it is binding, efficacious and of full force" (*Three Degrees of Glory*, 8).

DOCTRINE AND COVENANTS 76:54
What is "the church of the Firstborn"?

All those who faithfully live the Savior's gospel are "begotten" of him and considered "the church of the Firstborn" (see Mosiah 5:5–7; D&C 93:21–22). Unfortunately, not all members of the earthly Church qualify to be included with those righteous souls who are worthy of the celestial kingdom.

DOCTRINE AND COVENANTS 76:57
How was Melchizedek "after the order of Enoch"?

Joseph Smith's translation of Genesis 14 indicates how Melchizedek was "after the order of Enoch." Verse 34 indicates that Melchizedek followed Enoch's example, leading a Zion-like community that obtained a place in heaven. The Lord further explained that both Melchizedek and Enoch were "after the order of the Only Begotten Son" (D&C 76:57). This relationship was reflected in the original name of the higher priesthood (see D&C 107:3).

DOCTRINE AND COVENANTS 76:58–59
What is the difference between "gods" and "God's" in these verses?

"They are gods" is an affirmation that all of our Father's children who qualify for exaltation may become like him (see D&C 76:94–95). Even though "all things are theirs," they have received this inheritance only through the merits of Christ, so they are truly his. The Savior, in turn, received his power and glory from the Father. Hence we depend on, or belong to, Christ, and he belongs to his Father—he is "God's" (v. 59).

"Those who have been born unto God through obedience to the Gospel," declared the First Presidency, "may by valiant devotion to righteousness obtain exaltation and even reach the status of Godhood. . . . Yet, though they be Gods they are still subject to Jesus Christ as their Father in this exalted relationship" (Clark, *Messages of the First Presidency,* 5:31).

DOCTRINE AND COVENANTS 76:70–71
What do "celestial" and "terrestrial" actually mean?

Celestial means "heavenly" or "pertaining to the heavens." *Terrestrial* means "earthly" or "of the earth." The words do not refer to the location of these kingdoms but to their relative condition. Likewise Doctrine and Covenants 76 does not say that the celestial kingdom will be on the sun and the terrestrial on the moon but rather that the brilliance of the sun exceeds that of the moon, just as the glory of the celestial is greater than that of the terrestrial. A later revelation (see D&C 88:17–20, 25–26) clarifies that our celestial kingdom will be on this sanctified earth.

DOCTRINE AND COVENANTS 76:72–74
Why should we do temple work for the dead if those who receive the gospel in the spirit world can inherit only the terrestrial kingdom?

Many of those who receive the gospel in the spirit world will likely inherit the terrestrial kingdom. Those who qualify for that kingdom are described as "honorable" but "not valiant" in living the gospel (D&C 76:75, 79). Unfortunately there are Church members today who fit that description.

Yet there will be exceptions to this generalization. A remarkable vision of the celestial kingdom tells us that "all who have died without a knowledge of this gospel, who would have received it if they had been permitted to tarry, shall be heirs of the celestial kingdom" (D&C 137:7). These individuals are among those who receive the gospel in the spirit world. What determines the kingdom one inherits, then, is not when the gospel is received but how it is lived.

Those who accept the gospel in the spirit world have been promised that someone among their posterity will receive the gospel on earth and perform needed ordinances in their behalf. {See D&C 2:2.} We are that posterity. Hence, among our ancestors are faithful individuals who are worthy of the celestial kingdom and who are depending on our help to reach it.

DOCTRINE AND COVENANTS 76:77
Will Jesus live in the terrestrial kingdom?

As a member of the Godhead, Christ will dwell in the celestial kingdom (see D&C 76:62). The promise that the terrestrial "receive of the presence of the Son" means that he may visit there. Those in the telestial kingdom will have an even less direct relationship with the Godhead. {See D&C 76:86–88.}

DOCTRINE AND COVENANTS 76:81
What is the origin of the name "telestial"?

In contrast to *celestial* and *terrestrial*, which have meanings commonly used in our language, *telestial* is found uniquely in writings relating to latter-day revelation. This name appears to be related to the Greek *telos*, meaning "end" or "completion." Paul explained that there will be an orderly sequence in resurrections, beginning with that of Christ and continuing until the *telos*, or "end" (see 1 Corinthians 15:21–24). Those individuals who have earned the right to live in the telestial kingdom will be the last going to a kingdom of glory to be resurrected.

The name *telestial* may also be related to the prefix *tele-*, meaning "far off" or "distant." The telestial kingdom will be the kingdom of glory most removed from the presence and glory of God.

DOCTRINE AND COVENANTS 76:82
In what sense do the people of the telestial kingdom "receive not the gospel"?

Because all will have the opportunity to receive the gospel, the people of the telestial kingdom apparently choose not to do so. The scriptures testify that "every knee shall bow" and "every tongue shall confess" before the Lord (Romans 14:11; Isaiah 45:23). Even telestial inhabitants will have to acknowledge who Jesus Christ is (see D&C 76:110). But being basically sinful people (see D&C 76:103), they never make his gospel a part of their lives.

DOCTRINE AND COVENANTS 76:84
Is the telestial kingdom the same place as perdition or hell?

Reading the context of a scripture often clarifies its meaning. In this case the preceding verse, Doctrine and Covenants 76:83, indicates that those going to the telestial kingdom have not committed the unpardonable sin of denying the Holy Ghost and hence are not sons of perdition. {See D&C 76:31–35.} The following verse, number 85, clarifies that the "hell" into which they have been cast is only a temporary condition from which they will eventually be released (compare D&C 76:105–6 and Alma 40:11–14). Writers in the Book of Mormon sometimes used the word *hell* in reference to the spirit prison (see 2 Nephi 9:11–13, for example). The temporary torment suffered by telestial candidates in the spirit prison foreshadows the torment to be experienced eternally only by the sons of perdition.

DOCTRINE AND COVENANTS 76:86–88
How do those in the telestial kingdom receive the Holy Ghost "through the ministration of the terrestrial"?

Elder Orson Pratt explained that those in the terrestrial glory cannot ascend to the celestial kingdom. "Their intelligence and knowledge have not prepared and adapted them to dwell with those who reign in celestial glory, consequently they can not even be angels in that glory. They have not obeyed the law that pertains to that glory, and hence they could not abide it. But will there be blessings administered to them by those who dwell in celestial glory? Yes, angels will be sent forth from the celestial world to minister to those who inherit the glory of the moon, bearing messages of joy and peace and of all that which is calculated to exalt, to redeem and ennoble those who have been resurrected into a terrestrial glory. They can receive the Spirit of the Lord there, and the ministration of angels there" (in *Journal of Discourses*, 15:322).

Likewise, individuals from the terrestrial kingdom are permitted to minister to the telestial. Whereas those in the celestial world enjoy the fulness of the Father's glory, and those in the terrestrial may receive visitations from the Son, those in the telestial glory receive the influence of the Holy Ghost—and that, only indirectly—by means of visitors from the terrestrial degree.

DOCTRINE AND COVENANTS 76:96–98
Aren't there variations of glory within each of the kingdoms?

Doctrine and Covenants 76:98 specifically tells us that there are variations in the telestial glory, and we are likewise told that there are three levels of glory within the celestial kingdom (see D&C 131:1–4). From this information we may suppose that variations also exist in the terrestrial glory. The statement that the glory of each kingdom "is one" means that it is of a nature or kind distinct from the others.

DOCTRINE AND COVENANTS 76:99–100

Why do followers of these great religious leaders inherit only the telestial kingdom?

People may say that they follow Christ, but the following verses make clear that they "received not the gospel, neither the testimony of Jesus, neither the prophets" but actually are sinners (D&C 76:101–3). {See D&C 76:82.} Hence the telestial kingdom, the least of the degrees of glory, is a fit reward for them. One must do more than merely claim to be a follower of the Savior.

DOCTRINE AND COVENANTS 76:112

Will there be progress from one kingdom to another?

The concept of eternal progression may imply the possibility of progressing from one kingdom to another. Doctrinal teachings, however, suggest otherwise.

First, those who do not enter celestial marriage (an ordinance that must be received either personally during mortality or vicariously in the spirit world) can never be exalted, though they may become ministering angels in the celestial kingdom (see D&C 131:1–4; 132:15–16).

Second, we are resurrected with the body suited specifically for the glory we are worthy to receive. We cannot endure a higher glory for which our body is not prepared.

Third, the Lord has decreed that heirs of the telestial kingdom can never go where God and Christ are (see D&C 76:112). Elder Melvin J. Ballard elaborated on that restriction: "Those whose lives have entitled them to Terrestrial Glory can never gain Celestial Glory. One who gains possession of the lowest degree of Telestial Glory may ultimately arise to the highest degree of that glory, but no provision has been made for promotion from one glory to another" (*Three Degrees of Glory*, 35).

Fourth, counting on the possibility of progressing from kingdom to kingdom may lead us to procrastinate our repentance. That would undermine the importance of this life as the time for preparing to meet God (see Alma 34:32–34).

INSTRUCTIONS AND PROPHECIES

DOCTRINE AND COVENANTS 77 THROUGH 87

The revelations recorded in Doctrine and Covenants 77 through 87 were all given during 1832. They treat a variety of subjects, including the Revelation of John, the organization of the united order, the oath and covenant of the priesthood, and a prophecy on war.

DOCTRINE AND COVENANTS 77:2
Is our physical appearance in the likeness of our spirit or does it reflect inherited family traits?

Just as our physical heredity can blend traits from our father's and mother's sides of our ancestry, so can all of this merge with our spirit heritage.

DOCTRINE AND COVENANTS 77:12
When was man created, on the sixth or the seventh day?

The accounts in the Bible and the Pearl of Great Price record the creation of man as the crowning event of the sixth day (see Genesis 1:24–31; Moses 2:24–31; Abraham 4:24–31). Yet the revelation in Doctrine and Covenants 77 parallels mankind's creation with events that occur "in the beginning of the seventh thousand years."

One could argue that there is not much difference between the end of the sixth and the beginning of the seventh day. The book of Moses, however, may give a more satisfying answer. After giving an account of the six days of creation and of the Lord's resting on the seventh, this scripture reminds us that there were not yet living creatures on earth because they had only been created spiritually in heaven. At that point God "formed man from the dust of the ground" (Moses 3:5–7). That physical creation is probably the one spoken of by the Lord in Doctrine and Covenants 77:12. Note that the wording there is more like the description of the physical creation in Moses 3:7 than it is like the account of the earlier spiritual creation in Moses 2:27.

94

DOCTRINE AND COVENANTS 77:12–13
What do these verses suggest about the time of the Lord's second coming?

Some have supposed that there is to be exactly six thousand years from the Fall to the Second Advent, but a careful reading of these verses suggests otherwise. Doctrine and Covenants 77:12 declares that "in [not at] the beginning of the seventh thousand years," Christ will complete his work, preparing the way "before the time of his coming." Verse 13 explains that events described in Revelation 9 are to occur after the seventh period of a thousand years begins but before Christ appears. Thus estimates of the time of his advent based on these verses must be more tentative and probably later than some have supposed.

DOCTRINE AND COVENANTS 78:3–5
What was the united order?

In the revelation recorded in Doctrine and Covenants 78, the Lord called some of the leaders of the Church to unite by covenant to form what became known as the "united order" (D&C 104:1), or "united firm." This was an administrative body to coordinate and operate various business enterprises related to the law of consecration.

The phrase "united order" has also frequently been used as a synonym for "law of consecration." Cooperative ventures in Utah during the 1870s were also called "united orders" but were not the same as the law of consecration.

DOCTRINE AND COVENANTS 78:16
Who is Michael?

Michael is Adam, "the ancient of days" (D&C 27:11), who, as the patriarchal head of the human family, holds "the keys of salvation" under the direction of the Lord Jesus Christ. The name *Michael* literally means "one who is like God."

DOCTRINE AND COVENANTS 78:20
Who is "Son Ahman"?

"Ahman" is the name of the Father in the pure language of Adam, explained Elder Orson Pratt. "Son Ahman" is the name of the Son, and "sons Ahman" is the designation for the remainder of God's children (in *Journal of Discourses,* 2:342).

DOCTRINE AND COVENANTS 79:1
Why can the gospel be described as "glad tidings of great joy"?

The word *gospel* literally means "good news," that through Christ's atonement we can overcome our sins and once again be worthy to live in God's presence. {See D&C 33:10–12.}

DOCTRINE AND COVENANTS 82:3, 7–10
What will be taken into account when we are judged?

The Lord has decreed that obedience brings blessings and disobedience results in punishment (see D&C 82:10; 130:20–21; Alma 42:22). Other factors will also be considered in the Judgment. The Savior will take into account the level of our understanding (see D&C 82:3; Luke 12:47–48; Alma 9:23). Not all transgressions will result in punishment. The Lord has given the wonderful promise that if we repent of our sins, he will forgive them and "remember them no more" (D&C 58:42). The opposite, however, is also true. If a righteous person turns to sin, his former good deeds cannot save him (see D&C 82:7; Ezekiel 18:24; 33:12–16). It is not enough to be good now, but we must also endure in faithfulness to the end (see 2 Nephi 31:19–20).

DOCTRINE AND COVENANTS 84:4–5
How can the prophecy be fulfilled that the temple in the New Jerusalem would be built "in this generation"?

The word *generation* may have different meanings. Often it refers to the time between the birth of parents and that of their children, but it sometimes refers to those born during a given period of time. The followers of Granville Hedrick, who owned the temple lot in Missouri, interpreted "generation" to mean one hundred years and so believed the temple had to be built before 1932, a century after the revelation in Doctrine and Covenants 84 was received.

President Joseph Fielding Smith cited the Savior's allusion to "an evil and adulterous generation" (Matthew 12:39) and concluded that "this did not have reference to a period of years, but to a period of wickedness." He therefore reasoned, "A generation may mean the time of this present dispensation" (*Church History and Modern Revelation*, 1:337). If that definition is correct, it would mean the temple must be built during "this generation," that is, the dispensation of the fulness of times.

DOCTRINE AND COVENANTS 84:16

Why is the priesthood lineage here traced through Abel rather than through Seth as it is in Doctrine and Covenants 107:41–43?

Doctrine and Covenants 84 affirms that Moses' priesthood could be traced back to Adam. Verses 15–16 do not mention each individual in the early part of this priesthood line but simply testify that the priesthood was passed down "through the lineage of their fathers." Doctrine and Covenants 107 serves a different purpose, emphasizing that the office of patriarch was to be passed down from father to son. Because Abel had been killed, Seth was the person who actually ordained his fifth great-grandson, Lamech. That may explain why Seth, rather than Abel, is named in this priesthood lineage.

DOCTRINE AND COVENANTS 84:19–22

What are "the mysteries of the kingdom" and "the power of godliness"?

In his two great revelations on priesthood, the Lord declares that the higher priesthood holds the "keys of the mysteries of the kingdom." These mysteries include sacred truths that are known only by revelation: to have "the knowledge of God" (D&C 84:19), "to have the heavens opened," and to "enjoy the communion and presence of God the Father and Jesus" (D&C 107:19). In an earlier revelation Jesus Christ indicated that other sacred mysteries include "my will concerning all things pertaining to my kingdom," the "wonders of eternity," and "things to come" (D&C 76:7–8). The "power of godliness"—the ability to acquire godlike attributes and qualify to be in his presence—is made fully available only through the ordinances of the Melchizedek Priesthood (D&C 84:20–21).

DOCTRINE AND COVENANTS 84:21–22

How could Joseph Smith see God before receiving the priesthood?

"We cannot tie the hands of the Lord," President Joseph Fielding Smith taught. "The Father and the Son appeared to the Prophet Joseph Smith before the Church was organized and the priesthood restored to the earth. Under those conditions the Lord could appear to one who sought for light as he did in the case of Joseph Smith.

"Now that the Church is organized, and the power of the priesthood is here, no one can see the face of God, even the Father, without the blessings of the gospel and the authority of the priesthood" (*Doctrines of Salvation,* 1:4).

Joseph Smith declared: "Every man who has a calling to minister to the inhabitants of the world was ordained to that very purpose in the Grand Council of heaven before this world was. I suppose that I was ordained to this very office in that Grand Council" (*Teachings of the Prophet Joseph Smith,* 365). In a sense, then, the Prophet may have had the required authority through this foreordination.

DOCTRINE AND COVENANTS 84:29
Isn't "bishop" an office in the Aaronic Priesthood?

The office of bishop is the presiding office of the Aaronic Priesthood. This entire priesthood, with the bishop at its head, may be regarded as an appendage to the Melchizedek Priesthood (see D&C 84:29; 107:5). The subordinate offices of teacher and deacon, on the other hand, are identified as appendages within the lesser priesthood (see D&C 84:30).

DOCTRINE AND COVENANTS 84:31–32
Who are the sons of Moses and of Aaron, and what offering and sacrifice will they make?

Doctrine and Covenants 84:6–30 may be regarded as a long parenthetical explanation of the nature, history, and structure of the two orders of priesthood. Verse 31 then brings us back to the main flow of the revelation, and verse 32 picks up the thought originally introduced at the beginning of verse 6. The following verses then explain how those who faithfully magnify their calling become the "sons of Levi." {See D&C 84:33–41).} Those who honor their callings in the Melchizedek and Aaronic Priesthoods become in a figurative sense the sons of Moses and of Aaron, respectively.

Although literal members of the tribe of Levi will offer a sacrifice as a part of the "restitution of all things," the "offering" most commonly made by the sons of Moses and Aaron will be their faithful priesthood service. {See D&C 13.}

DOCTRINE AND COVENANTS 84:33–41
Under the "oath and covenant of the priesthood," what promises do we and God make?

"There is no exaltation in the kingdom of God without the fullness of the priesthood," affirmed President Joseph Fielding Smith, "and every man who receives the Melchizedek Priesthood does so with an oath and a covenant that he shall be exalted.

"The covenant on man's part is that he will magnify his calling in the priesthood, and that he will live by every word that proceedeth forth from the mouth of God, and that he will keep the commandments.

"The covenant on the Lord's part is that if man does as he promises, then all that the Father hath shall be given unto him; and this is such a solemn and important promise that the Lord swears with an oath that it shall come to pass" (in Conference Report, Apr. 1970, 58–59).

Elder Marion G. Romney taught: "With . . . 'eternal life . . . the greatest of all the gifts of God' (D&C 14:7) depending upon it, it is of utmost importance that we keep clearly in mind what the magnifying of our callings in the priesthood requires of us. I am persuaded that it requires at least the following three things:

"1. That we obtain a knowledge of the gospel.

"2. That we comply in our personal living with the standards of the gospel.

"3. That we give dedicated service" (*Improvement Era*, June 1962, 416).

DOCTRINE AND COVENANTS 84:45–46
What is the Spirit of Christ?

The Spirit of Christ is God's power by which the universe was created and by which "all things are governed." It emanates "from the presence of God to fill the immensity of space" (D&C 88:6–13). Like the more powerful and direct influence of the Holy Ghost, the light of Christ may be known as "the Spirit of God" or the "light of truth." Unlike the direct ministration of the Holy Ghost, which is more specific and is received only by certain worthy individuals, the spirit of Christ "enlighteneth every man through the world, that hearkeneth to the voice of the Spirit" (D&C 84:46). Specifically, the Spirit of Christ helps us discern good from evil (see Moroni 7:15–19) and is an important part of what the world calls "conscience." It helps prepare the honest in heart to receive the gospel and the confirming witness through the Holy Ghost.

DOCTRINE AND COVENANTS 84:54–57
Why are we under condemnation if we neglect the Book of Mormon?

President Ezra Taft Benson cited Doctrine and Covenants 84 as he emphasized the importance of the Book of Mormon (see, for example, *Ensign*, May 1975, 65; May 1986, 82; Nov. 1986, 4). Because the chief mission of the Book of Mormon is to bear witness of Jesus Christ, our faith in the Savior might be weakened without the spiritual support of this volume of scripture. Then, as our devotion to the Lord and our determination to live his gospel are lessened, we deprive ourselves of spiritual blessings and thus bring upon ourselves a kind of condemnation.

DOCTRINE AND COVENANTS 84:77–88
How can we develop the kind of relationship with the Lord described in these verses?

There should be a close relationship between the Lord and his servants. He regards us as his friends and is even aware of such an insignificant occurrence as a hair falling from our heads. The Master promises to inspire us with the right words to speak in any situation— if we have done our part to be prepared. His promise to go before our face, to be on our right and on our left, to bless us with his Spirit, and to place his angels round about us suggest a very close and personal working relationship. He has told us how to cultivate such a relationship: we must serve him and keep all his commandments (see D&C 42:29). We must make the effort to draw closer to him (see D&C 88:63). We must always be humble and prayerful (see D&C 112:10). The ultimate promise he makes to us is that we can behold his face and know that he lives. {See D&C 67:10.}

DOCTRINE AND COVENANTS 84:78–84
Shouldn't we prepare for the future?

When the Savior gave a discourse in ancient America that was like the Sermon on the Mount he had given in the Old World, he carefully designated which portions were directed only to the Twelve and which were for the whole multitude. The command to be unconcerned with material preparations was given specifically to the Twelve (see 3 Nephi 13:25–34; 14:1). Those who are called into full-time Church service receive support from the Church. {See D&C 42:70–73.} Likewise, missionaries should he prepared so they need not worry about their financial support while serving. {See D&C 24:18.}

DOCTRINE AND COVENANTS 84:107
How does this procedure work today?

Aaronic Priesthood youth, as well as Church members in general, can play an important role in helping missionaries do their work more efficiently. We can "friendship" our neighbors and associates and, when the time is right, arrange for them to receive the missionary discussions. After converts are baptized, we can play an equally significant role as we fellowship them and help them truly "join the Church."

DOCTRINE AND COVENANTS 84:108–10
How have these verses influenced Church organization and activities?

Beginning in the 1960s, Church leaders emphasized what they called "priesthood correlation." After quoting Doctrine and Covenants 84:108–10, Elder Harold B. Lee declared: "This significant statement meant clearly that, first, each organization was to have its specific function, that it was not to usurp the field of the other which would be like the eye saying to the hand, 'I have no need of thee'; second, that each subdivision is of equal importance in the work of salvation, just as each part of the physical body is essential to the complete human being; . . . or in other words, that within the framework of the Lord's plan of organization for the salvation of his children, the Church will perform as a perfectly organized human body with every member functioning as it was intended" (in Conference Report, Oct. 1962, 72).

Today, priesthood executive committees and correlation councils meet at local and general levels to better coordinate programs and activities under priesthood direction and make sure they are meeting the needs of individual members and families.

DOCTRINE AND COVENANTS 85:7
Was the "one mighty and strong" ever sent?

In Doctrine and Covenants 85:3–5, the Lord warned that individuals going to Zion (Jackson County, Missouri) who refused to live the law of consecration would not have their names recorded among the names of those worthy to receive blessings. Because Bishop Edward Partridge was lax in dealing with such individuals, the Lord threatened to send "one mighty and strong" to set his affairs in order (D&C 85:7).

Through the years many apostates have come forward, claiming the right to lead the Church as "the one mighty and strong" the Lord had promised. In 1905, however, the First Presidency noted that Bishop Partridge had repented and so the Lord's threat did not need to be carried out. "If, however, there are those who will still insist that the prophecy concerning the coming of 'one mighty and strong' is still to be regarded as relating to the future," the First Presidency instructed, "let the Latter-day Saints know that he will be a future bishop of the Church who will be with the Saints in Zion, Jackson County, Missouri" (Clark, *Messages of the First Presidency,* 4:118).

Some apostate groups profess to hold the "high priesthood" and, therefore, claim to be above the jurisdiction of the organized Church. Nevertheless, verse 11 in section 85 makes even those bearing the "high priesthood" subject to the Church's discipline.

DOCTRINE AND COVENANTS 86:1–7
Why does this interpretation of the parable of the sower differ from that found in Matthew 13?

Doctrine and Covenants 86 places the Lord's parable of the wheat and tares (see Matthew 13:24–30, 36–43) in the context of the latter days (compare JST Matthew 13:41 with D&C 101:64–75). During the Savior's earthly ministry he himself was the sower of the good seed (see Matthew 13:37), whereas in the latter-days, this task is accomplished by his servants (see D&C 86:2). The Church being driven into the wilderness (see D&C 86:3) describes the apostasy; the Restoration is likened to "the Church being called forth out of the wilderness" (D&C 33:5). In Doctrine and Covenants 86:5–7, the Lord declared that he was holding his angels back from cleansing out the wicked because his kingdom was still young. Years later, however, President Wilford Woodruff wrote that the time had come for the gathering out of the tares and that the Lord had released his angels to "reap down the earth" (in Conference Report, Oct. 1896; quoted in Smith, *Church History and Modern Revelation,* 365).

DOCTRINE AND COVENANTS 87
Which aspects of this prophecy on war have been fulfilled?

Certain aspects of the prophecy in Doctrine and Covenants 87 saw one specific fulfillment with the civil war in the United States in the 1860s. That war began in South Carolina (see v. 1); the division was North against South (see v. 3) rather than the manufacturing Northeast against the agricultural Northwest and South—the division in the nation that prevailed at the time this revelation was received. The Confederacy called on Great Britain for help (see v. 3), and Southern slaves rebelled against their masters (see v. 4).

Other aspects of this prophecy are related to wars in general. World wars have characterized the twentieth century (see vv. 2–3), and oppressed peoples in many parts of the world have thrown off the yoke of totalitarian governments or other forms of dictatorship (see v. 4).

Descendants of Father Lehi, long oppressed by the Gentiles, have often fought back (see v. 5). Still other facets of the Lord's prophecy (see vv. 6–7) are yet to be fulfilled.

DOCTRINE AND COVENANTS 87:8
In the midst of these wars, how can we "stand in holy places"?

Once again the Lord directs his people to stand apart from wickedness. {See D&C 45:32.} He has promised that by so doing the faithful will be blessed in the midst of prophesied latter-day tribulations (see D&C 63:34; 115:6).

SPIRITUAL AND TEMPORAL MATTERS

DOCTRINE AND COVENANTS 88 THROUGH 96

The revelations recorded in Doctrine and Covenants 88 through 96 were given in 1832 and 1833. During this time the temporal concerns of the Church ranged from personal health (see D&C 89) to raising funds for the construction of sacred buildings in Kirtland (see D&C 94–96). At the same time the Lord sought to lift the Saints' thoughts to eternal spiritual matters. In the revelation recorded in section 88 he dealt with such topics as education, the Holy Spirit of promise, the last days, and the resurrection. Then, in section 93, he described how we can obtain a fulness of light and truth and be glorified even as he is.

DOCTRINE AND COVENANTS 88
Why was this revelation called "the Olive Leaf"?

Doctrine and Covenants 88 was received when there had been contentions among some of the Latter-day Saints. Perhaps the Prophet hoped that the lofty concepts it contained might divert the Saints' thoughts from their insignificant passing differences to those great eternal truths that should unite them. In this way the "leaf . . . plucked from the Tree of Paradise" might truly become a "message of peace" and joy to the Church (Smith, *History of the Church*, 1:316).

DOCTRINE AND COVENANTS 88:3–4
Why may the Holy Ghost be called "the Holy Spirit of promise"?

The Holy Ghost was the subject of an important promise the Savior made to his disciples just before his atoning sacrifice (see John 14:16–17, 26). The Spirit conveys to us the most significant promise we could hope to receive while in this life (see D&C 88:3–4). {**See D&C 76:53.**}

DOCTRINE AND COVENANTS 88:14–16
Why is the resurrection "the redemption of the soul"?

Even though *soul* is often used as a synonym for *spirit,* Doctrine and Covenants 88:15 gives a more precise definition. The soul is actually composed of two elements: the spirit and the body. When the spirit and the body come together at mortal birth, the soul is created. Then, when they are parted by physical death, the soul is temporarily dissolved. The resurrection eventually reunites the spirit and the body, which never again will be separated (see Alma 11:45; 40:23). The resurrection is literally "the redemption of the soul."

DOCTRINE AND COVENANTS 88:22
What exactly is the "celestial law"?

The celestial law spoken of in Doctrine and Covenants 88 includes the principles and ordinances of the gospel that prepare us to inherit celestial glory.

DOCTRINE AND COVENANTS 88:25
How can such lifeless objects as our planet keep a celestial law?

Doctrine and Covenants 88:25 is not the only scripture that attributes lifelike actions to inanimate objects. Enoch learned that "the earth mourned" because of the sins of its inhabitants (see Moses 7:48–49), and the apostle Paul likewise declared that "the whole creation groaneth and travaileth" (Romans 8:22).

In 1909 the First Presidency explained that God also created lower forms of animal life "but He did not make them in His own image, nor endow them with Godlike reason and intelligence. Nevertheless, the whole animal creation will be perfected and perpetuated in the Hereafter, each class in its 'distinct order or sphere,' and will enjoy 'eternal felicity'" (*Improvement Era,* Jan. 1909, 81).

Elder John A. Widtsoe carried this concept further to include even inanimate objects: Joseph Smith suggested that "energy in the universe is a form of intelligence" not understood by man. "Some form of life resides in all matter, though of an order wholly different from the organized intelligence of men or higher living things. . . . Hence, everything in the universe is alive. The differences among rock, plant, beast, and man are due to the amount and organization of the life element" (*Joseph Smith*, 149–50). Elder Orson Pratt declared that there is "a degree of intelligence even in these materials. There does not seem to be any agency so far as we naturally comprehend it." If there is, "it seems to be very obedient" (in *Journal of Discourses*, 21:233). Nephi likewise acknowledged that natural objects obey God's commands but lamented that we are "even less than the dust of the earth" because of our frequent disobedience (see Helaman 12:8–17).

DOCTRINE AND COVENANTS 88:27–32
What is the difference between celestial and other kinds of bodies?

All resurrected bodies will be physically perfect. Alma testified that "even a hair of the head shall not be lost; but all things shall be restored to their proper and perfect frame" (Alma 40:23; see also 11:44).

Nevertheless, our bodies will be suited for the degree of glory that we are qualified to inherit. If we have kept the celestial law, assured Elder Joseph Fielding Smith, "the Father has promised us that through our faithfulness we shall be blessed with the fulness of his kingdom. In other words we will have the privilege of becoming like him. To become like him we must have all the powers of godhood; thus a man and his wife when glorified will have spirit children" (*Doctrines of Salvation*, 2:48).

DOCTRINE AND COVENANTS 88:34–35
Why does obedience to God's laws perfect and sanctify us?

Because we are God's children, our Father knows us perfectly and he understands what will bring us lasting happiness and joy. He knows the path we must follow and has given laws, or commandments, to help keep us on that path. The effect of his laws might be likened to a railroad track that follows the route surveyors previously determined to be the best course to a given destination. As long as the train stays on the rails, its forward motion is maintained; but if it jumps the track, its progress comes to a sudden halt.

Many in the world regard obedience to law as inhibiting or confining. The Lord, on the other hand, has equated righteousness with liberty and labeled sin as entangling (see D&C 88:86). Elder John A. Widtsoe testified: "Human experience forbids the thought that a settled

106

purpose may be achieved under a hit or miss system. A progressive existence is derived from obedience to the laws of progress, and can be won in no other way. No candidate for salvation can escape obedience to the laws of progress which form the framework of the plan of salvation" (*Program of the Church,* 211).

DOCTRINE AND COVENANTS 88:65
How can we avoid praying for the wrong things?

In the revelation in which the Savior outlined the gifts of the Spirit, he stated that the Holy Ghost can direct us to pray for the right things (see D&C 46:30; compare 50:30). "Therefore, we should not be too insistent" in demanding of the Father our own wishes, cautioned President Joseph Fielding Smith, "but should pray earnestly . . . to know the will of the Lord" (*Church History and Modern Revelation,* 1:371). If, like Nephi of old, we fearlessly and selflessly keep the commandments, the Lord might be able to give us the same remarkable promise made to him: "All things shall be done unto thee according to thy word, for thou shalt not ask that which is contrary to my will" (Helaman 10:4–5).

DOCTRINE AND COVENANTS 88:76–80
Why is education important? What should we study? How?

Many in the world have justified obtaining education on the grounds that it enables us to earn higher incomes. The Lord, however, suggested a more lofty reason: that we might be better prepared to serve (see D&C 88:80). To this end he directed us to study a wide variety of subjects (compare v. 79 with 90:15 and 93:53). Nevertheless, Elder John A. Widtsoe acknowledged, "God does not require all His servants to become doctors, or professors, or even profound students of these subjects, but He expects them to know enough of these things to be able to magnify their calling as His ambassadors to the world" (*Priesthood and Church Government,* 55–56).

Our learning of these secular subjects, however, must be bathed in the light of the gospel. "Now, there's only one reason why this church is in the school business," asserted Elder Harold B. Lee. "We're not in the education field just to teach science and philosophy and athletics. We are in the educational world today because we want to teach the spiritual side along with the intellectual side, that when we have graduates from this institution [Brigham Young University], please

God that they might come out with a degree in science, or philosophy, or languages, or whatnot, but still having faith in the living God" (*Teachings of Harold B. Lee*, 352).

The Lord put "the doctrine of the kingdom" first in his list of subjects we should study (D&C 88:77–78). President Brigham Young pointed out that "there are a great many branches of education: some go to college to learn languages, some to study law, some to study physic [medicine], and some to study astronomy, and various other branches of science. We want every branch of science taught in this place that is taught in the world. But our favourite study is that branch which particularly belongs to the Elders of Israel—namely, theology. Every Elder should become a profound theologian" (in *Journal of Discourses*, 6:317).

The Master instructed that we should learn "by study and also by faith" (D&C 88:76, 118). Regardless of what subject we are studying, we need to do all we can to gain an understanding of it and prepare ourselves to receive the additional insights available by revelation from our Father who knows all things. "The things of God cannot be learned solely by study and reason," Elder Dallin H. Oaks taught. "Despite their essential and beneficial uses, the methods of study and reason are insufficient as ways of approaching God and understanding the doctrines of his gospel" (*Lord's Way*, 56).

DOCTRINE AND COVENANTS 88:93
What is the "great sign"?

"The sign of the coming of the Son of Man—what is it? We do not know," answered Elder Bruce R. McConkie (*Millennial Messiah*, 418). When that sign appears, Joseph Smith prophesied, the world "will say it is a planet, a comet, etc. But the Son of Man will come as the sign of the coming of the Son of Man, which will be as the light of the morning cometh out of the east" (*Teachings of the Prophet Joseph Smith*, 286).

In response to a report that a certain man had already seen this sign "in the clouds one morning about sunrise," the Prophet declared that it would not appear until after the calamities mentioned in Doctrine and Covenants 88:87 had occurred (*History of the Church*, 5:291). "When the sign appears, God will make its meaning known to the Prophet, Seer and Revelator who at that time may be at the head of the Church, and through him to His people and the world in general" (Smith and Sjodahl, *Commentary*, 560).

DOCTRINE AND COVENANTS 88:97-102
Who are the various groups mentioned in these verses?

The "first fruits" of the resurrection mentioned in Doctrine and Covenants 88:97 and 98 are those worthy of the celestial kingdom. Those who receive the gospel in the spirit world and who are "Christ's at his coming" (v. 99) will inherit the terrestrial glory. Those described in verses 100 through 102 who are worthy only of the telestial kingdom or who became sons of perdition on earth will also appear to be judged, but they will not receive their resurrection until the end of the Millennium (Smith, *Church History and Modern Revelation*, 1:369).

DOCTRINE AND COVENANTS 88:118
What are the "best books"?

Certainly "the best books" include the standard works, but they also include much more. {See D&C 88:76–80.} Elder Richard L. Evans counseled, "Never become narrowly educated, but broadly so, feeding all sides of yourselves, reading and becoming acquainted with good books, with great minds and great men of the past; becoming acquainted with scripture and reading scripture itself" (in Conference Report, Apr. 1961, 75).

DOCTRINE AND COVENANTS 88:119
What is the "house" referred to here?

In Doctrine and Covenants 88:127 the Lord clarified that in this passage he was speaking of a place where the school of the prophets should meet. Three years later, when the Kirtland Temple was completed, the instructions in this verse were applied to the temple (see D&C 109:6–10). We could well strive to live in such a way that the qualities listed in Doctrine and Covenants 88:119 might also more fully characterize our own homes.

DOCTRINE AND COVENANTS 88:121
Is it really wrong to laugh?

The Lord has directed us to live the gospel and keep his commandments "with a glad heart and a cheerful countenance" (D&C 59:15; compare 19:39; 123:17; Proverbs 15:13; Revelation 19:7). Nevertheless, he cautioned us to do these things without "idle thoughts" or "excess of laughter" (D&C 88:69). The instructions in

Doctrine and Covenants 88 were given as part of the Lord's directive to hold "solemn assemblies." In such sacred gatherings boisterous laughter is not appropriate.

"I do not believe the Lord intends and desires that we should pull a long face and look sanctimonious and hypocritical," counseled Elder Joseph Fielding Smith (in Conference Report, Oct. 1916, 70). Nevertheless, he declared, "amusement, laughter, [and] light-mindedness, are all out of place in the sacrament meetings of the Latter-day Saints" (in Conference Report, Oct. 1929, 62).

DOCTRINE AND COVENANTS 89:1-2
Isn't the Word of Wisdom binding on Church members?

The introductory verses of Doctrine and Covenants 89 indicate that this revelation was to be sent out "not by commandment or constraint" (v. 2). "The reason undoubtedly why the Word of Wisdom was given as not by 'commandment or restraint,'" suggested President Joseph F. Smith, "was that at that time, at least, if it had been given as a commandment it would have brought every man, addicted to the use of these noxious things, under condemnation; so the Lord was merciful and gave them a chance to overcome, before He brought them under the law" (in Conference Report, Oct. 1913, 14). Nevertheless, "when members of the Church had had time to be taught the import of the revelation," noted President Boyd K. Packer, "succeeding Presidents of the Church declared it to be a commandment. And it was accepted by the Church as such" (Ensign, May 1996, 17).

Still, section 89 had always identified the "Word of Wisdom as a "revelation . . . showing forth the order and will of God" (v. 2). A few months earlier, the Master had decreed: "And now I give unto you a commandment . . . to give diligent heed to the words of eternal life. For you shall live by every word that proceedeth forth from the mouth of God" (D&C 84:43–44). There seems to be little practical distinction between a "commandment" and a revelation of God's will. Furthermore, the Lord explained that he was giving this revelation "for the benefit" of the Saints, describing it as a "principle with promise" (D&C 89:1, 3). The concluding verses of section 89 outline the beneficial results promised to those who faithfully observe the principles in this revelation.

"It isn't unusual—indeed, it is expected," observed Elder Richard L. Evans, "that the maker of any machine should send a set of instructions on how best to use it, how best to care for it; and this our Father in heaven has done for us, mentally, morally, physically, spiritually. In the gospel are instructions from our Maker on how to care for and keep ourselves at our best for the purpose for which we were brought into being.

"As to the physical side: More than a century ago, a prophet of God simply said that some things are not good for man. Now, knowledgeable and intelligent men of science and medicine also say so. . . .

"Some say there is no moral question on how we physically live our lives. But isn't it a moral question to abuse what God has given? And what a waste to abuse any useful creation of any kind. If someone were to give us a finely working watch, wouldn't it be foolish, indeed irrational, to put into it that which would corrode and defeat its purpose?

"We have only one body. It is irreplaceable, indispensable, sacred. It has to last a mortal lifetime. With it and the spirit within, we think, we plan, we work, we feel, we live our mortal lives.

"It is a miracle and most amazing: the housing for the spirit, the mind, the intelligence of man; the instrument through which we think and plan and pursue life's purpose.

"Don't dissipate it; don't impair any part of it. Keep it clean and functioning. Don't quibble about words, about what is counsel and what is commandment" (in Conference Report, Apr. 1967, 9–10).

DOCTRINE AND COVENANTS 89:2
Isn't the Word of Wisdom a "spiritual" commandment?

Obviously, refraining from the use of liquor, tobacco, and other harmful substances has temporal benefits. Still, the Lord has declared that he has never given a law which is "temporal" only; hence, the Word of Wisdom is essentially spiritual. {See D&C 29:34.}

DOCTRINE AND COVENANTS 89:9
Which "hot drinks" should we avoid?

The Prophet Joseph Smith declared that "tea and coffee are what the Lord meant when he said 'hot drinks'" (in Widtsoe and Widtsoe, *Word of Wisdom*, 85–86). The Lord has described as "slothful" servants those who wait to be "commanded in all things" (D&C 58:26). We could well seek to identify other harmful substances we should avoid. Concerning cola drinks, for example, Bishop Vaughn J. Featherstone reminded us: "The leaders of the Church have advised, and we do now specifically advise, against use of any drink containing harmful habit-forming drugs" (in Conference Report, Apr. 1975, 102).

"Members write in asking if this thing or that is against the Word of Wisdom," observed President Boyd K. Packer. "It's well known that tea, coffee, liquor, and tobacco are against it. It has not been spelled out in more detail. Rather, we teach the principle together with the promised blessings. There are many habit-forming, addictive things that one can drink or chew or inhale or inject which injure both body and spirit which are not mentioned in the revelation" (*Ensign*, May 1996, 17).

We should be cautious in sharing our own conclusions and opinions with others. Only the prophet has the stewardship to define what is or is not against the Word of Wisdom.

DOCTRINE AND COVENANTS 89:13
Should we eat meat?

In an earlier revelation, the Lord declared that "the beasts of the field and the fowls of the air, and that which cometh of the earth, is ordained for the use of man for food and for raiment" (D&C 49:19). Doctrine and Covenants 89:12–15 clarified that meat should be eaten only sparingly. This counsel is consistent with recent research that has raised concerns about too much cholesterol and fat in our diets.

DOCTRINE AND COVENANTS 90:6
Who holds keys, and what are they?

"Keys" are the right to preside and the power to direct in the Lord's work. Stake presidents, bishops, and elders quorum presidents—but not their counselors—hold keys. Each member of the Quorum of the Twelve Apostles receives all the keys, which are held "in suspension, pending a time when he might become the senior apostle and the President" (Spencer W. Kimball, in Conference Report, Apr. 1970, 118). The president of the Church is the only one who is authorized to exercise the keys in full (see D&C 132:7). The revelation in Doctrine and Covenants 90 explains that counselors in the First Presidency share to an extent in holding the keys, but they are still subject to the administration and direction of the prophet (see vv. 6–9).

DOCTRINE AND COVENANTS 90:25

What is the meaning of the counsel to "let your families be small"?

The counsel to "let your families be small" has nothing to do with limiting the number of children, because the Lord was speaking of "those who do not belong to your families." The Lord in particular addressed his "aged servant," Joseph Smith Sr., who was sixty-one years old, well beyond the usual age of having children. In addition, the term *family* had been used among Sidney Rigdon's Campbellite congregation to mean a cooperative group consisting of several conventional families.

The practice had developed among the Saints to extend hospitality to the numerous visitors and newcomers arriving in Kirtland. Doctrine and Covenants 90:26 specifically warned them not to dissipate their goods on "those that are not worthy," who might take advantage of such hospitality.

DOCTRINE AND COVENANTS 91

How can we apply the Lord's instructions about the Apocrypha?

The Apocrypha is a collection of fourteen books included in the Catholic Bible but not in most Protestant Bibles. Those books help bridge the four-hundred-year gap between the Old and New Testaments. The Lord declared that the Apocrypha contains many things that are true along with many other things which are not (see D&C 91:1–2). Because that description may be applied to almost every non-scriptural work we may read, we may profit generally from the Lord's admonition to read with the discerning power of his Spirit (see vv. 4–5).

DOCTRINE AND COVENANTS 92:2

How can we be "lively" members?

A dictionary published about the time this revelation was received defines *lively* as "vigorous, active, strong, or energetic" (Webster, *American Dictionary*). Those are qualities all of us should take into our Church assignments. To increase our effect for good, we should take to heart such counsel as "let your light so shine" (Matthew 5:16), "be anxiously engaged" (D&C 58:27), "magnify" your calling (D&C 84:33), and so on.

DOCTRINE AND COVENANTS 93:1
What is our responsibility to seek this extraordinary blessing?

The exalted blessing of seeing God's face may come to us in this mortal life or it may be realized after death. {See D&C 67:10.} "I have learned," gratefully acknowledged President Spencer W. Kimball, "that where there is a prayerful heart, a hungering after righteousness, a forsaking of sins, and obedience to the commandments of God, the Lord pours out more and more light until there is finally power to pierce the heavenly veil and to know more than man knows. A person of such righteousness has the priceless promise that one day he shall see the Lord's face and know that he is" (*Ensign*, Mar. 1980, 4).

DOCTRINE AND COVENANTS 93:6–18
Is this the record of John the Baptist or of John the Apostle?

In the opening chapter of his gospel, John the Apostle bore witness of Christ's glorious role since the beginning (see John 1:1–14). He also quoted the testimony or "record" of John the Baptist (John 1:15, 19–34). Doctrine and Covenants 93 seems to be quoting from both John the Apostle (see vv. 8–10) and from John the Baptist (see vv. 15–16).

DOCTRINE AND COVENANTS 93:12–13, 20
How do we receive "grace for grace" and then continue "from grace to grace"?

John testified that we have received of God's fulness "grace for grace" (John 1:16). That phrase may have several meanings. The dictionary in the LDS edition of the Bible defines *grace* as "divine means of help or strength." Perhaps John means that we receive this help "for," or because of, God's goodness and power. The Jerusalem Bible's translation states that "we have, all of us, received—one gift replacing another," the gospel of Christ replacing the law of Moses (p. 1243). The New International Version translates this message in John as, "We have all received one blessing after another" (p. 1593).

Latter-day Saint scholar Richard Draper has suggested another possibility. "To receive grace for grace is to receive assistance on the condition of giving assistance.

"Apparently, it was necessary for the Lord to grow through this process. In order to do so, he first received grace, or divine assistance

114

from the Father. This grace he extended to his brethren. As he did so he received even more grace. The process continued until he eventually received a fulness of the glory of the Father" ("Light, Truth, and Grace," 37–38).

Significantly, we too must receive "grace for grace" (D&C 93:20). Once we have begun receiving God's gifts, our challenge is to ascend "from grace to grace," or from one gift to another. Through continued righteousness we progress from one level of holiness to another until we receive a fulness of Godlike attributes.

DOCTRINE AND COVENANTS 93:29–33
What is the ultimate source of our agency?

Some theologians have insisted that God created all things ex nihilo (out of nothing). That would make him totally responsible for everything that exists—both good and evil. Doctrine and Covenants 93, however, affirms that the physical "elements are eternal" and that intelligence "is independent in that sphere in which God has placed it, to act for itself." Man likewise "was not created or made" and so is also eternal. Hence both matter and our intelligence have had an eternal, independent, existence. "Behold," declared the Lord, "here is the agency of man" (D&C 93:31).

Our Father's plan was based on our inherent agency. "The Lord gave to man his free agency in the pre-existence," testified President Joseph Fielding Smith. "This great gift of agency, that is the privilege given to man to make his own choice, has never been revoked, and it never will be" (*Answers to Gospel Questions*, 2:20). With agency comes responsibility and accountability. If we misuse it, we come "under condemnation" (D&C 93:32). If, on the other hand, we take advantage of its opportunities, our potential is limitless.

DOCTRINE AND COVENANTS 93:36
What is the meaning of the often-quoted phrase
"the glory of God is intelligence"?

Some have assumed that this phrase refers only to gaining an education. For Latter-day Saints, however, the word *intelligence* may have two distinct meanings: (1) academic ability or mental capacity, and (2) that part of our being that has existed from the beginning. The context of this scripture suggests that it refers to the second of these meanings. Notice how Doctrine and Covenants 93:36 equates God's glory with "light and truth," and verse 29 indicates that these were attributes of man "in the beginning." In other words, we had the same qualities that constitute God's glory, but we had them in only a small degree whereas he has them in full. The essential message of section 93 is that by keeping God's commandments we can receive "truth and light" until we have them in full and are glorified (vv. 20, 28). On the other hand, we are cautioned that Satan "taketh away light and truth through disobedience" (v. 39).

Even though this revelation describes a broad process of spiritual growth, seeking learning has an important part in the process. "Truth," one of the key attributes of God's glory, is defined as a "knowledge of things as they are and as they were, and as they are to come" (v. 24). In an earlier revelation the Master directed us to "seek learning, even by study and also by faith" (D&C 88:118). {See D&C 88:76–80; 88:118.} A later revelation emphasizes that "if a person gains more knowledge and intelligence in this life through his diligence and obedience than another, he will have so much the advantage in the world to come" (D&C 130:19).

Elder John A. Widtsoe distinguished between intelligence and mere learning. "It often happens that a person of limited knowledge but who earnestly and prayerfully obeys the law, rises to a higher intelligence or wisdom, than one of vast Gospel learning who does not comply in his daily life with the requirements of the Gospel. Obedience to law is a mark of intelligence" (in Conference Report, Apr. 1938, 50).

DOCTRINE AND COVENANTS 94:3–9
What was the "house for the presidency"? Was it the Kirtland Temple?

At the heart of the city of Kirtland were to be the temple and two other sacred buildings. On the first lot south of the temple was to be a house for the presidency, and on the second lot was to be a house for the publication of God's word (see D&C 94:3, 10). All three of these buildings were to have the same dimensions (compare vv. 4, 11 with 95:15).

The latter two structures—the buildings for the presidency and the press—were not to be built until the Lord gave further instruction (see D&C 94:16). This direction was not given before the Saints were forced to flee from Kirtland. On the other hand, less than a month after Doctrine and Covenants 94 had been received, the Lord did give further instruction concerning the design and building of his temple (see D&C 95:8–17). Within a few weeks of these revelations the Prophet drew up his plat for the city of Zion, in which he called for not three but twenty-four sacred structures to serve as "houses of worship, schools, etc." at the city's center (*History of the Church,* 1:358).

DOCTRINE AND COVENANTS 95:7
Who is the "Lord of Sabaoth"?

Sabaoth is the plural form of the Hebrew word *Sabah,* meaning "hosts or armies." The phrase "Lord of Sabaoth" emphasizes the power and majesty of the Lord Jesus Christ. This verse highlights his role as the Creator.

Perhaps the reason *Sabaoth* is not translated is that this title is used similarly to the way it was employed in two biblical passages that use this term in reference to Christ's role as judge. Compare Doctrine and Covenants 87:8; 88:2; and 95:7 with Romans 9:29 and James 5:4.

10

YEARS OF TRIAL AND TRIUMPH

DOCTRINE AND COVENANTS 97 THROUGH 112

The difficulties the Saints experienced during the summer of 1833 culminated that fall in their being driven from their homes in Jackson County, Missouri. The next summer an expedition of more than two hundred men from Ohio and nearby areas failed to help their brethren regain their lost property. Nevertheless, great strides forward were taken with the organization of the first Quorum of the Twelve Apostles and the dedication of the Kirtland Temple. With keys restored at the Kirtland Temple, the Twelve opened the Church's first overseas mission in England. Doctrine and Covenants 97 through 112 records the revelations received between 1833 and 1837.

DOCTRINE AND COVENANTS 98:16

Does the Lord's command to "renounce war" mean we should become pacifists?

Pacifism is the opposition to the use of force under any circumstances. A pacifist therefore refuses for reasons of conscience to participate in any kind of military action. In Doctrine and Covenants 98, in which the Lord commands us to "renounce war," he indicates there are circumstances in which we are justified in going to war (see vv. 33–36). The Nephites were instructed anciently that they should not start wars for selfish gain but to fight "even to the shedding of blood if it were necessary" in defense of their homes, their freedoms, and their religion (Alma 48:14; see also 43:45–47).

Only a few weeks after the outbreak of World War II, the First Presidency reminded the Church that we must obey constitutional law (see D&C 98:4–7): "When, therefore, constitutional law, obedient to these principles, calls the manhood of the Church into the armed service of any country to which they owe allegiance, their highest civic duty requires that they meet that call. If, harkening to that call and obeying those in command over them, they shall take the lives of those who fight against them, that will not make of them murderers, nor subject them to the penalty that God has prescribed for those who kill. . . . For it would be a cruel God that would punish His children as moral sinners for acts done by them as the innocent instrumentalities of a sovereign whom He had told them to obey and whose will they were powerless to resist" (in Conference Report, Apr. 1942, 94–95).

DOCTRINE AND COVENANTS 98:23–48
How many times are we expected to forgive?

The Savior instructed Peter that he should forgive those who offended him "seventy times seven" (Matthew 18:21–22). Latter-day Saint scholar Sidney B. Sperry pointed out: "The Master's answer to Peter, uttered in the form of common Oriental overstatement, did not mean that one was to forgive his brother exactly four hundred and ninety times. The spirit of it was that a man should have a lot of forgiveness in his heart" (*Doctrine and Covenants Compendium*, 500). A latter-day revelation tells us that we should forgive always (see D&C 64:9–10). {See D&C 64:9–10.}

A superficial reading of Doctrine and Covenants 98, however, may give the impression that we are expected to forgive only three times. Verses 23 through 27 require that we forgive our enemies at least three times and emphasize that we should do so "patiently." If our enemy comes against us a fourth time, he is in our hands; but, even then, "if thou wilt spare him, thou shalt be rewarded for thy righteousness" (v. 30). Such forbearance would give offenders time to reconsider their actions and perhaps repent.

This revelation was given to the Saints at the time they were being violently driven from Jackson County, Missouri. Even though they would be blessed for maintaining an attitude of forgiveness, they were not expected to stand by without seeking to defend themselves. "If [thine enemy] has sought thy life, and thy life is endangered by him, thine enemy is in thine hands and thou art justified" (v. 31). Still, "the Lord counselled the Saints to seek redress, not revenge" (Otten and Caldwell, *Sacred Truths*, 2:167).

In the revelation in Doctrine and Covenants 98, the Lord likewise admonishes all of us not to limit the number of times we are willing to work with transgressors even when they are not seeking forgiveness

119

(see vv. 39–45). When action must be taken against the unrepentant, it should be done in the Lord's way (see v. 44; compare 42:88–92).

DOCTRINE AND COVENANTS 101:2–6
What caused the Saints' difficulties?

Historians have pointed out that there were various sources of tension between the Mormons and other Missourians, including the following: the Saints were often abolitionists from the North whereas other residents of Jackson County were slaveholders from the South; most Missourians considered faith in continuing revelation through a living prophet to be strange; and the Mormons patronized their own businesses and boasted that Jackson County was to become their Zion, and so forth.

There may be truth in such explanations, but the Lord pinpointed quite a different reason for the difficulties: the Saints themselves were guilty of transgressions, disunity, lustfulness, greed; and they were slow to hearken to the Lord (see D&C 101:2–6; 103:4; 105:3–4). These deficiencies were in marked contrast to the qualities required of those who would build Zion: they must be "of one heart and one mind" and dwell "in righteousness" (Moses 7:18), and they must also be pure in heart (see D&C 97:21). Hence, the Saints needed to be chastened to help them become worthy.

DOCTRINE AND COVENANTS 101:20–21
Has this shift in the pattern of gathering taken place?

The Lord indicates in Doctrine and Covenants 101 that the gathering of his Saints is an important part of their preparation for his coming in glory. As anticipated in verses 20 and 21, the emphasis in the Church has shifted to establishing stakes where the Saints are living rather than gathering the Saints into just one place. This change came with the dawning of the twentieth century. {See D&C 29:7–8.}

DOCTRINE AND COVENANTS 101:24–34
When will these wonderful conditions come to pass?

Doctrine and Covenants 101:24–34 is one of the best descriptions anywhere in scripture of the conditions that will prevail during the Millennium. Verses 24 and 25 refer to the time when "the earth will be renewed and receive its paradisiacal glory" (Article of Faith 10) and when those who are not worthy to live in this condition will be burned as stubble (see Malachi 4:1). {See **D&C 63:20–21**.} The peaceful conditions spoken of in Doctrine and Covenants 101:26 were beautifully described by Isaiah (see Isaiah 11:6–9). Because of the people's righteousness, the Lord makes the same promise to them that he made to Nephi of old (compare v. 27 with Helaman 10:4–5).

Doctrine and Covenants 101:28 testifies that Satan will be bound (compare Revelation 20:2–3). We have been taught that he will be bound because of the righteousness of the people and because Christ will reign in their midst (see 1 Nephi 22:26).

Doctrine and Covenants 101:29–31 explains that even though people will die during the Millennium, there will not be death as we know it. All will live until they are old (compare Isaiah 65:20–22 and D&C 63:50) and then not be buried in the ground but rather be "changed in the twinkling of an eye" from mortality to immortality. This promise is comparable to that given to those who become translated beings. {See **D&C 7:2**.}

Finally, Doctrine and Covenants 101:32–34 promises that the Lord "will reveal all things," including even how the earth was created. Knowing that this marvelous revelation is coming, we should now be patient and refrain from counterproductive speculation on such matters.

DOCTRINE AND COVENANTS 102
What is the purpose of Church courts?

Elder Robert L. Simpson explained the purpose of Church courts, now called disciplinary councils: "Priesthood courts of the Church are not courts of retribution. They are courts of love." Their purpose is to help the transgressor to take "the first giant step back" (in Conference Report, Apr. 1972, 32, 33).

A second purpose of these councils is to protect the Church and its members. Those who would corrupt others by promoting false doctrines or sinful conduct may need to be removed from Church membership. To preserve its good name, the Church sometimes must take action against transgressors, particularly when their misdeeds have received widespread attention.

There are three principal disciplinary councils in the Church. First, at the ward level, the bishop and his counselors form the council having original jurisdiction in most cases. Second, the stake presidency and the high council may consider appeals from the bishop's court or they may initiate action in certain cases. Doctrine and Covenants 102:1–23 outlines how this judicial body is to function. Third, the First Presidency constitutes the earthly tribunal of final appeal. There are also special disciplinary councils in missions and others to meet unique circumstances (see D&C 102:24–34).

Church discipline has several forms. Probation may involve some restrictions in Church activity. Disfellowshipment means that the individual cannot hold a calling or be invited to pray or speak in meetings but is encouraged to attend. Excommunication is the ultimate penalty in which a person loses membership in the Church together with all priesthood and temple blessings; following thorough repentance the individual may be readmitted to the Church through rebaptism. In all cases the individual is encouraged to repent, and the Church reaches out to help in this process.

DOCTRINE AND COVENANTS 103
What was the response to this call?

The Missouri Saints' difficulties culminated with their being driven out of Jackson County during the late fall of 1833. In February of the following year this revelation called for up to five hundred volunteers to help restore the refugees to their homes, and recruiting efforts were launched for what became known as "Zion's Camp." That group began its long march from New Portage, Ohio, on 8 May 1834. After it crossed the Mississippi River its numerical strength peaked at "207 men, 11 women, 11 children, and 25 baggage wagons" (*Church History in the Fulness of Times*, 143). By the time Zion's Camp reached Missouri, both Church leaders and the state's governor concluded that conditions were not favorable for calling out the militia to assist the Saints in returning to their lands in Jackson County.

Though the avowed purpose of the camp was not realized, "it was definitely not an exercise in futility, but rather served as the forge in which the Lord tempered the steel of many of his early leaders" (*Doctrine and Covenants Student Manual*, 258). Many future Church leaders demonstrated their faith and devotion to the cause of Zion during this difficult march. For several weeks, the Prophet personally instructed these men as they camped and marched together. Nine of the original Twelve Apostles and all of the original Quorum of Seventy were chosen from among those who had responded to the call to join Zion's Camp. Furthermore, this lengthy cross-country trek provided valuable experience to Church leaders who a dozen years later would have to direct the forced evacuation of men, women, and children from Nauvoo under much more difficult circumstances.

DOCTRINE AND COVENANTS 105:31
How is the Lord's "army" measuring up?

Before Zion can be established, the Lord's "army," or Church, must have the necessary strength in numbers and in quality. The Church's worldwide growth means that it is rapidly becoming very great. {See D&C 65:2–6.} But just how many members the Lord requires has not been revealed, but the larger the Church grows, the closer it approaches the needed level.

To be "sanctified," the quality the Lord requires for his army, means being holy and worthy in every way. Because sanctification is a personal process, it is difficult to measure. Nevertheless, increased attendance at meetings, paying of tithes, and temple activity do reflect a person's greater faithfulness.

DOCTRINE AND COVENANTS 107:19
What are "the mysteries of the kingdom of heaven"?

As he had done in his other great revelation on priesthood, the Lord again affirmed that the higher priesthood holds "the key of the mysteries of the kingdom, even the key of the knowledge of God." {See D&C 84:19–22.}

DOCTRINE AND COVENANTS 107:22
By what "body" is the First Presidency chosen?

President Harold B. Lee explained that "body" in Doctrine and Covenants 107:22 "has been interpreted to mean the entire Quorum of the Twelve" (*Teachings of Harold B. Lee,* 535). After the death of a prophet, the apostles meet fasting in the Salt Lake Temple and prayerfully consider who should become the new president of the Church. Since the martyrdom of Joseph Smith, the Quorum of the Twelve has consistently followed the pattern of nominating the senior apostle, the one who has served for the longest continuous time in the Quorum of the Twelve.

DOCTRINE AND COVENANTS 107:22-26
How can the First Presidency, the Quorum of the Twelve Apostles, and the Seventy be "equal in authority"?

The members of the First Presidency hold all the keys and direct the affairs of all other quorums and the Lord's kingdom throughout the world. The Quorum of the Twelve Apostles also holds the keys but functions "under the direction of the Presidency of the Church" (D&C 107:33).

"I want here to correct an impression that has grown up to some extent among the people," taught President Joseph F. Smith, "and that is, that the Twelve Apostles possess equal authority with the First Presidency in the Church. This is correct when there is no other Presidency but the Twelve Apostles; but so long as there are three presiding Elders who possess the presiding authority in the Church, the authority of the Twelve Apostles is not equal to theirs. If it were so, there would be two equal authorities and two equal quorums in the Priesthood, running parallel, and that could not be, because there must be a head" (Elders Journal, 1 Nov. 1906, 43).

Similarly, the Seventy function "under the direction of the Twelve" (D&C 107:34). They would become "equal in authority" only if both the First Presidency and the Quorum of the Twelve were dissolved.

DOCTRINE AND COVENANTS 107:23
What does it mean to be a "special witness"?

President Joseph Fielding Smith observed: "The question frequently arises, 'Is it necessary for the members of the Council of the Twelve to see the Savior in order to be an apostle?' It is their privilege to see him if occasion requires, but the Lord has taught that there is a stronger witness than seeing a personage. . . .

" . . . seeing, even the Savior, does not leave as deep an impression in the mind as does the testimony of the Holy Ghost to the spirit . . .

" . . . It is where Spirit speaks to spirit, and the imprint upon the soul is far more difficult to erase" (in Doxey, Latter-day Prophets and the Doctrine and Covenants, 4:28-29).

Elder Boyd K. Packer likewise recalled: "Occasionally during the past year I have been asked a . . . curious, almost an idle, question about the qualifications to stand as a witness for Christ. The question they ask is, 'Have you seen Him?'

"I have not asked that question of others, but I have heard them answer it—but not when they were asked. They have answered it under the prompting of the Spirit, on sacred occasions, when 'the Spirit beareth record.' (D&C 1:39.)

"I have heard another testify: 'I know that God lives; I know that the Lord lives. And more than that, I know the Lord'" (in Conference Report, Apr. 1971, 123–24).

Not only is seeing the Lord in person unnecessary to being a special witness but it is also insufficient. Elder Dallin H. Oaks pointed out that even though the early apostles had personally associated with the Savior, "he cautioned them that their witnessing would be after they had received the Holy Ghost (see Acts 1:8; see also Luke 24:49).

"An eye witness was not enough. Even the witness and testimony of the original Apostles had to be rooted in the testimony of the Holy Ghost" (in Conference Report, Oct. 1990, 36).

Although the Twelve were described as "special witnesses" (D&C 107:23), the seventy were to be "especial witnesses" (v. 25). *Special* and *especial* are synonymous, and so no distinction is intended.

DOCTRINE AND COVENANTS 107:36–37
In what sense are stake high councils "equal in authority" to the First Presidency and the Twelve?

Just as the Quorum of the Twelve functions under the direction of the First Presidency and the Seventy under the Twelve, so do stake leaders function under the direction of these General Authorities. The stake presidency and high council are charged to give spiritual leadership in their stake as do the presiding quorums for the whole Church.

On 3 July 1834, after organizing the Church's second high council in Zion (Missouri), the Prophet Joseph Smith instructed that through this council "the will of the Lord might be known on all important occasions, in the building up of Zion, and establishing truth in the earth" (*History of the Church*, 2:124).

This responsibility of the high council in Zion is carried out today by more than two thousand standing high councils in their respective stakes of Zion. {See D&C 124:133–40.}

DOCTRINE AND COVENANTS 107:39
What are "evangelical ministers"?

"I am not sure that I know precisely why the words 'evangelical ministers' were used rather than the word 'patriarchs,'" said Elder

Joseph Fielding Smith. "It seems, however, significant to me that the term here used suggests very definitely the spiritual nature of the patriarchal office" (in Conference Report, Oct. 1944, 110).

The word *evangel* means "gospel"; hence, an evangelist is one who proclaims the gospel. In a very real sense, patriarchal blessings are personal revelations of the gospel, emphasizing particular promises, cautions, and admonitions relevant to the individual recipient. The Prophet Joseph Smith taught: "An Evangelist is a Patriarch, even the oldest man of the blood of Joseph or of the seed of Abraham. Wherever the Church of Christ is established in the earth, there should be a Patriarch for the benefit of the posterity of the Saints, as it was with Jacob in giving his patriarchal blessing unto his sons, etc." (*Teachings of the Prophet Joseph Smith*, 151).

DOCTRINE AND COVENANTS 107:41–43
Why is the priesthood lineage here traced through Seth rather than through Abel as it is in Doctrine and Covenants 84:16?

The two lineages serve different purposes. Here the emphasis is on who personally conferred the priesthood. {See D&C 84:16.}

DOCTRINE AND COVENANTS 107:58
To what other revelation was the Lord referring?

A manuscript copy of a revelation dated November 1831 corresponds to Doctrine and Covenants 107:59–107, which seems to be the earlier revelation to which the Lord refers in verse 58. The references between verses 61 and 88 to literal descendants of Aaron and the bishopric and the material in verses 93 through 98 on the Seventy were added when this earlier revelation was merged into section 107 (Woodford, *Historical Development of the Doctrine and Covenants*, 1403). This means that the material on the duties of quorum presidencies was known as early as 1831, rather than 1835.

DOCTRINE AND COVENANTS 107:93
What is the vision concerning the Seventy?

The precise content of this vision is not known, but it may have been alluded to in a history of the Seventy written by Joseph Young, the first senior president of that quorum. On Sunday, 8 February 1835, the Prophet Joseph Smith invited Brigham and Joseph Young to meet with him privately. After describing a vision "of the state and condition of those men who died in Zion's Camp, in Missouri," the Prophet instructed Brigham Young to have the brethren assemble the following Saturday when he would "appoint twelve special witnesses, to open the door of the gospel to foreign nations," indicating that Brigham would be one of them.

"He then turned to Elder Joseph Young with quite an earnestness, as though the vision of his mind was extended still further, and addressing him, said: 'Brother Joseph, the Lord has made you President of the Seventies'" (Young, *History of the Organization of the Seventies*, 1–2). The Quorum of the Twelve Apostles was organized on 14 February 1835, and the Seventy were chosen two weeks later.

DOCTRINE AND COVENANTS 109:34
To whom was this prayer addressed?

The Savior taught that we should pray to the Father in his name (see John 16:23; 3 Nephi 18:19–20). Nevertheless, when Jesus was standing in the midst of his disciples, they appropriately "prayed," or addressed their praises, directly to him (see 3 Nephi 19:18).

The dedication of the Kirtland Temple was another such special situation. The revealed dedicatory prayer formally followed the usual pattern: "Now we ask thee, Holy Father, in the name of Jesus Christ . . ." (D&C 109:4). Still, verse 34 seems to be addressing the Lord Jesus Christ, to whom the house was being dedicated.

Elder Bruce R. McConkie suggested a slightly different interpretation: "We pray to the Father, and because our answers come from Jehovah, we sometimes give forth accolades of praise to him, in the language of prayer, which those untutored in the things of the Spirit might mistakenly interpret to be prayers to the Son and not the Father" (*Promised Messiah*, 337).

DOCTRINE AND COVENANTS 109:79–80
To what exultant "shout" do these verses refer?

The sacred Hosanna Shout has been part of every temple dedication. The entire congregation stands and three times joyously shouts "Hosanna, Hosanna, Hosanna, to God and the Lamb! Amen, Amen, and Amen." These words are reflected in Doctrine and Covenants 109:79–80 as well as in William W. Phelps' hymn "The Spirit of God." Like the "Hosanna Shout" itself, this great hymn, written in anticipation of the Kirtland Temple's dedication, has been part of every temple dedication since.

Hosanna is the Hebrew for "save, we pray." In ancient times the shout was often rendered out of doors, accompanied with the waving of leafy branches from trees. One such occasion was Christ's triumphal entry into Jerusalem when throngs went out to meet him shouting "Hosanna!" and waving palm fronds (see John 12:12–13). Interestingly, the Kirtland Temple was dedicated on Palm Sunday, 27 March 1836, so the "Hosanna Shout" was given for the first time in this dispensation on the very day when Christians around the world were commemorating that ancient shout of "Hosanna!"

DOCTRINE AND COVENANTS 110:11
How have the keys of gathering been exercised in the present dispensation?

On 3 April 1836 Moses bestowed "the keys of the gathering of Israel from the four parts of the earth" (D&C 110:11). Since that time Latter-day Saint missionaries have carried the gospel around the world, and the receptive descendants of Israel have been gathered into the Lord's Church. The first overseas mission, in Great Britain, was opened in 1837, the year after Moses' appearance. The Jews began their return to the Holy Land in the mid-nineteenth century, and in 1948 they organized the nation of Israel.

Moses also conferred the power to lead "the ten tribes from the land of the north." This grand event (see Jeremiah 16:14–15), which will closely precede the Lord's second coming, is still future.

DOCTRINE AND COVENANTS 110:12
Who was Elias, and what authority did he restore?

"What prophet this Elias is that was sent to restore these keys is not definitely known," acknowledged President Joseph Fielding Smith (*Church History and Modern Revelation,* 2:49). The title *Elias* designates a forerunner commissioned to prepare the way, and it has been applied to several forerunners, most notably John the Baptist (see Luke 1:17; Matthew 17:11–13). The Elias who appeared in the Kirtland Temple restored "the dispensation of the gospel of Abraham" (D&C 110:12), so he likely lived in the days of that great prophet. Some have speculated that he was Melchizedek, but President Joseph Fielding Smith believed he was Noah. Joseph Smith taught that Noah was Gabriel, who stood second only to Adam in holding priesthood keys (*Teachings of the Prophet Joseph Smith,* 157). Gabriel was the messenger who appeared to Zacharias (see Luke 1:5–17) and who was identified in a latter-day revelation (see D&C 27:7) as Elias. Thus Noah is Gabriel who is Elias. Concluded President Smith, "This is the same Elias who held the keys of the dispensation of Abraham and who came to the Prophet Joseph Smith" in 1836 and restored those keys (*Answers to Gospel Questions,* 3:139–40). Noah lived just before Abraham's day and so would have been a fitting forerunner, or Elias, to the glorious Abrahamic dispensation.

The authority brought by Elias is described as "the dispensation of the gospel of Abraham" with the promise that "in us and our seed all generations after us should be blessed" (D&C 110:12). This promise is similar to the promise the Lord made to Abraham that through him "shall all the families of the earth be blessed, even with the blessings of the Gospel, which are the blessings of salvation, even of life eternal" (Abraham 2:11). The precise nature and extent of the keys bestowed by Elias are yet to be made known.

DOCTRINE AND COVENANTS 110:13–16
Why was Elijah chosen to restore certain keys?
How have they turned the hearts of the children to their fathers?

The sealing keys restored by Elijah are the power by which actions performed on earth will be "bound," or recognized, in heaven (Matthew 16:19). During his earthly ministry Elijah exercised priesthood powers to a remarkable degree—including sealing the heavens so that no rain would fall, multiplying the widow's meal and oil, restoring her son from death to life, and calling down fire from heaven (see 1 Kings 17–18)—and he was taken into heaven without tasting death (see 2 Kings 2). Joseph Smith taught that "Elijah was the last Prophet that held the keys of the priesthood" before the meridian of time (*Teachings of the Prophet Joseph Smith,* 172).

The restoration of the sealing keys was "to turn the hearts of the fathers to the children, and the children to the fathers" (D&C 110:15; compare Malachi 4:5–6 and D&C 2:2). Before the coming of Elijah in 1836, said Elder Joseph Fielding Smith, "there was no endeavor of any import to search the records of the dead. . . . There were no organizations or societies on the face of the earth, as far as I can learn, gathering records of the dead, before the year 1836. In 1837, however, one year later, Great Britain passed laws providing for and compelling the preservation of records of the dead. In the year 1844, the New England Historical and Genealogical Society was organized in Boston, and I think this was the first organization of the kind in the world. . . . The Spirit has taken hold of the people, not only in the Church but also of many who are not of the Church, and they, too, are searching the records, and compiling them" (in Conference Report, Apr. 1948, 133).

EXILES IN NORTHERN MISSOURI

DOCTRINE AND COVENANTS 113 THROUGH 123

The Saints faced opposition both in Missouri and in Ohio. Difficulties in Kirtland culminated with Joseph Smith and other faithful Saints fleeing for their lives early in 1838. By spring that year they had joined the exiles from Jackson and Clay Counties and began establishing Far West and other settlements in northern Missouri. Unfortunately, the break from persecution did not last very long. On 27 October 1838 Missouri governor Lilburn Boggs ordered that the Saints be exterminated or driven from the state. The Haun's Mill Massacre and Joseph Smith's arrest followed within a few days. Doctrine and Covenants 121, 122, and 123 are extracts from a lengthy letter written by the Prophet while he was confined at Liberty Jail. During this time the Lord revealed such important matters as the complete name of his Church (see D&C 115:4) and the law of tithing (see D&C 119:120).

DOCTRINE AND COVENANTS 113:3-6
Who are the "root" and the "rod" of Jesse?

In his great chapter on the last days and the Millennium, Isaiah speaks of a "rod," "stem," and "root of Jesse" (Isaiah 11:1, 10). We know that Jesse was the father of King David, and we learn by revelation that the "stem of Jesse" is Jesus Christ (D&C 113:1-2), but the identity of the "rod" and "root" are not as clearly stated (D&C 113:3-6).

Comparing what the Lord said about the "rod" and "root of Jesse" (D&C 113:4, 6) suggests that both refer to the same person. Unto him, declared the Lord, "rightly belongs the priesthood" (D&C 113:6). Who better fits this promise than does the Prophet Joseph Smith? reasoned Dr. Sidney B. Sperry. As the "'servant in the hands of Christ,' . . . Joseph

Smith fits naturally into Isaiah's prophecy, and it is easy to understand why Moroni quoted and explained Isaiah 11 to him" (*Improvement Era,* Oct. 1966, 869, 914). When Moroni appeared to Joseph Smith in 1823, he said that the prophecies in Isaiah 11 were "about to be fulfilled" (Joseph Smith–History 1:40). "That fulfillment began," suggested Dr. Kent Jackson of Brigham Young University, "at that very moment, when the Prophet began to receive the instruction and training that led to the restoration of all things. It will culminate in a glorious fulfillment—in the millennial reign of the Lord Jesus Christ" ("Revelations Concerning Isaiah," 333).

DOCTRINE AND COVENANTS 115:4
Has the Church always been known by this name?

When the kingdom of God was organized in 1830, it was known as "the Church of Christ" (D&C 20:1) or as "The Church of Jesus Christ." By 1834 *The Evening and Morning Star* observed, "As the members of this Church profess a belief in the truth of the Book of Mormon, the world, either out of contempt and ridicule, or to distinguish us from others, have been very lavish in bestowing the title of 'Mormonite.'" The *Star*'s editor was convinced that this "stigma" was the result of a "bitterness of feeling" and emphatically declared, "We do not accept the above title [Mormonite]" (*History of the Church,* 2:62–63 n).

Church members did not want to be guilty of being called by "the name of a man" (3 Nephi 27:8). Consequently, on 3 May 1834, the First Presidency and other Church leaders convened to seek inspiration on this matter. "After prayer, the conference proceeded to discuss the subject of names and appellations, when a motion was made by Sidney Rigdon, and seconded by Newel K. Whitney, that this Church be known hereafter by the name of 'The Church of the Latter-day Saints'" (*History of the Church,* 2:62–63). This name was consistent with the New Testament practice of referring to the early Christians as "saints" (see, for example, Romans 1:1–7; 1 Corinthians 1:1–2; Ephesians 1:1). This title suggests one who is holy—the word *saint* coming from the same root as *sanctified.* Nevertheless, one may be called a saint without one's being perfect, for as Paul explained, the central purpose of the Church is "for the perfecting of the saints, for the work of the ministry, for the edifying of the body of Christ" (Ephesians 4:12).

Elder B. H. Roberts noted that the record of the 1834 council was headed "Minutes of a Conference of the Elders of the Church of Christ." Therefore, "while the conference adopted the title 'The Church of the Latter-day Saints,' and the Church was for some years called by that name, it was not the intention to regard the Church as any other than the Church of Christ" (Smith, *History of the Church*, 2:62 n). It seems clear that these early Saints were not trying to abandon the name "Church of Jesus Christ" but rather were inspired to adopt a means of referring to themselves as something other than "Mormonites."

The revelation given in 1838 declared what the true name of the Church was to be: "For thus shall my church be called in the last days, even The Church of Jesus Christ of Latter-day Saints" (D&C 115:4). In this way the inspired description "Latter-day Saints" was added as a suffix to the essential designation "Church of Jesus Christ." The capitalized "The" affirms the Church's unique standing among all other organizations. {See D&C 1:30.}

"The name thus conferred," explained Elder James E. Talmage, "is a self-explanatory and exclusive title of distinction and authority. It is an epitome of the cardinal truths and of the philosophical basis of the system commonly called 'Mormonism'" (*Vitality of Mormonism*, 40). Elder B. H. Roberts wrote: "It is the 'Church of Jesus Christ.' It is the Lord's; He owns it, He organized it. . . . but it is an institution which also belongs to the Saints. . . . They have a conjoint ownership in it with Jesus Christ, which ownership is beautifully recognized in the latter part of the title" (Smith, *History of the Church*, 3:24 n).

DOCTRINE AND COVENANTS 116
What is the significance and meaning of "Adam-ondi-Ahman"?

Located in northern Missouri, the place called Adam-ondi-Ahman has been important during three distinct periods. First, just before his death, Adam gathered his righteous posterity together, blessed them, and gave them inspired instructions; the Lord also appeared and honored Adam as patriarch of the human family (see D&C 107:53–56). Next, during the later 1830s, Adam-ondi-Ahman was one of the Saints' larger settlements in northern Missouri. Finally, just before the Second Coming, another great council will be held at Adam-ondi-Ahman.

Elder Joseph Fielding Smith explained that the latter-day council at Adam-ondi-Ahman will be "of the greatest importance to this world. At that time there will be a transfer of authority from the usurper and impostor, Lucifer, to the rightful King, Jesus Christ. Judgment will be set and all who have held keys will make their reports and deliver their stewardships, as they shall be required. Adam will direct this judgment, and then he will make his report, as the one holding the keys for this earth, to his Superior Officer, Jesus Christ. Our Lord will then assume the reins of government; directions will be given to the Priesthood; and He, whose right it is to rule, will be installed officially by the voice of the Priesthood there assembled. This grand council of Priesthood will be composed, not only of those who are faithful who now dwell on this earth, but also of the prophets and apostles of old, who have had directing authority" (*Way to Perfection*, 291).

Concerning the meaning of Adam-ondi-Ahman, Elder Orson Pratt explained that "'Ahman' signifies God. The whole term means Valley of God, where Adam dwelt. It is in the original language spoken by Adam, as revealed to the Prophet Joseph" (in *Journal of Discourses*, 18:343). President Alvin R. Dyer suggested a slightly different interpretation. Because the keys of salvation were given through Adam, "we can understand the true meaning of the term 'Adam-ondi-Ahman'; or simply: from 'Ahman,' who is the Lord—'ondi,' meaning through Adam unto mankind" (in Conference Report, Oct. 1968, 109).

DOCTRINE AND COVENANTS 119:1, 3
Should we contribute a surplus before beginning to pay tithing?

The recipients of the revelation recorded in Doctrine and Covenants 119 had been living the law of consecration, which required them to give their surpluses to the bishop. Therefore, meeting that obligation was for them "the beginning of the tithing" (D&C 119:3). "In more recent times the Church has not called upon the members to give all their surplus property to the Church, but it has been the requirement according to the covenant, that they pay the tenth," wrote President Joseph Fielding Smith (*Church History and Modern Revelation*, 2:92).

DOCTRINE AND COVENANTS 119:2
Why should we pay tithing?

As is the case with other matters, there may be various levels of motivation. We should be eager to pay tithing simply because we love God and want to keep his commandments (see John 14:15; D&C 42:29).

We should regard tithing as an obligation. The Psalmist declared that "the earth is the Lord's" (Psalm 24:1). "We are not our own, we are bought with a price," asserted President Brigham Young. "We are the Lord's; our time, our talents, . . . and all there is on this earth that we have in our possession is the Lord's, and he requires one tenth of this for the building up of his kingdom" (*Discourses of Brigham Young*, 176). President George Albert Smith put it this way: "He places all in our hands, authorizing us to retain for our own use nine-tenths of it, and then He asks that we put His tenth where He directs, where He knows it will accomplish the most good in developing His Church" (in Conference Report, Apr. 1941, 28). Elder Marion G. Romney concluded: "It is apparent that tithing is a debt which everyone owes to the Lord for his use of the things that the Lord has made and given to him to use. It is a debt just as literally as the grocery bill, or a light bill, or any other duly incurred obligation. As a matter of fact, the Lord, to whom one owes tithing, is in a position of a preferred creditor. If there is not enough to pay all creditors, he should be paid first" (*Blessings of an Honest Tithe*, 4).

Elder Howard W. Hunter thought of our obligation to pay tithing in a rather unique way. While in law school he thought of various visual images to represent different kinds of stealing. "To represent the theory of embezzlement I thought of a nontithepayer. The Lord's share came into his hands lawfully, but he misappropriated it to his own use" (in Conference Report, Apr. 1964, 34).

Tithing might be regarded as "the Lord's law of revenue." Doctrine and Covenants 119:2 suggests some uses to which tithes rightfully might be put. In our day these sacred funds are used for such purposes as building chapels and temples, supporting stake and ward budgets as well as missionary and temple activities, helping those in need, and so forth.

The Lord has promised great blessings to those who pay tithing: "Bring ye all the tithes into the storehouse, that there may be meat in mine house, and prove me now herewith, saith the Lord of hosts, if I will not open you the windows of heaven, and pour you out a blessing, that there shall not be room enough to receive it" (Malachi 3:10).

Elder Reed Smoot testified: "I believe that the man who pays his honest tithing to God will not only be blessed by God himself, but that the nine-tenths will reach farther than would the ten-tenths if he did not obey that law" (in Conference Report, Oct. 1900, 7–8). Elder James E. Talmage believed that even "the soil can be sanctified by the tithing of its products." He was convinced that there is a relationship between the "elements and forces of nature and the actions of men" (in Conference Report, Oct. 1929, 68). "The law of tithing is the law of inheritance," declared Elder Melvin J. Ballard. "No man may hope or expect to have an inheritance on this celestial globe who has failed to pay his tithing" (in Conference Report, Oct. 1929, 51).

DOCTRINE AND COVENANTS 119:4
How should we calculate our tithing?

"Tithing means one-tenth," emphasized Elder John A. Widtsoe. "Those who give less do not really pay tithing; they are [only] lesser contributors to the Latter-day cause" (*Evidences and Reconciliations*, 285).

The Master stipulated that the Saints should "pay one-tenth of all their interest" (D&C 119:4). The First Presidency has explained that interest "is understood to mean income" (circular letter, 19 Mar. 1970). Elder Howard W. Hunter taught: "Interest means profit, compensation, increase. It is the wage of one employed, the profit from the operation of a business, the increase of one who grows or produces, or the income to a person from any other source" (in Conference Report, Apr. 1964, 35).

"When you are in doubt as to just how you should calculate your tithes," suggested Elder James E. Talmage, "reverse the terms as we sometimes do in solving complex mathematical problems, and suppose for the time being that the Lord had said this . . . : 'In order to show my love for my people, the faithful members of my Church, it is my will, saith the Lord, that each one shall receive from my storehouse, the storehouse of my Church, at regular intervals during the year, an amount equal to one-tenth of his income.' Now my dear brother, sit down and calculate how much the Lord owes you under that kind of law, and then go pay it to your bishop" (in Conference Report, Oct. 1928, 119).

DOCTRINE AND COVENANTS 119:4
When should we pay our tithing?

The word *annually* in this verse does not mean just once a year but rather suggests our continuing responsibility to pay tithing. Church leaders have counseled us to pay it as we receive our income. We should pay the Lord first. Lamentably, the way some people pay tithing may be described as follows: the Lord offers us ten apples with the request that we return only one to him. We should hand it back to him immediately, but often we eat our nine apples first, then look at the remaining apple longingly, and take a bite or two before reluctantly handing it to the Lord. The advantages of paying the Lord first should be obvious.

DOCTRINE AND COVENANTS 120
How does this council function today?

The *Encyclopedia of Mormonism* explains: "The Council on the Disposition of Tithes, consisting of the First Presidency of the Church, the Quorum of Twelve Apostles, and the Presiding Bishopric . . . meets regularly and oversees the expenditures of all Church funds world-wide. It approves budgets and financial strategy and establishes financial policy.

"Two subcommittees of the Council on the Disposition of Tithes are the Budget Committee and the Appropriations Committee. Both committees consist of the First Presidency, selected members of the Quorum of the Twelve Apostles, and members of the Presiding Bishopric.

"The Church Budget Office provides staff support to the First Presidency and gives overall administrative direction to the preparation of the annual Church budget. At the beginning of each annual budgeting cycle, budget guidelines are given to Church administrative department heads, international offices, missions, temples, and other units. Within these guidelines, budgets are constructed at the lowest levels of accountability and scrupulously reviewed through various levels of management and councils. The Budget Committee meets periodically to provide in-depth budget review and to formulate budget recommendations to the Council on the Disposition of Tithes" (Ludlow, *Encyclopedia of Mormonism*, 508).

Those who have been involved in these committees testify that the voice of the Lord has been sought diligently as directed by Doctrine and Covenants 120. Bishop Joseph L. Wirthlin, who served as a member of the Presiding Bishopric and was involved in these councils for nearly a quarter of a century, gratefully testified: "I have been inspired and thrilled by the careful appropriating of Church funds" (in Conference Report, Apr. 1953, 99).

DOCTRINE AND COVENANTS 121:37
Are ordinances performed by unworthy priesthood bearers invalid?

"As a result of unrighteousness, it is 'Amen to the priesthood' of a man," taught Elder Bruce R. McConkie, "meaning that his priesthood comes to an end, as far as being a power which would assure the bearer of eternal life is concerned" (*Mormon Doctrine*, 32). Thus, if a man becomes unrighteous, his unmagnified priesthood will become a source of personal condemnation rather than blessing.

Unworthiness impairs a man's ability to bless others through his priesthood. Nevertheless, if an unworthy person is called upon unknowingly to perform an ordinance, the ordinance is valid because the individual performs it not so much by his own authority as by his having been duly appointed as an agent for the Church. Basing the validity of ordinances on the worthiness of the officiator would inevitably raise questions and create confusion. Hence the efficacy of ordinances depends on the worthiness of those receiving them rather than on the worthiness of those performing them.

NAUVOO THE BEAUTIFUL

DOCTRINE AND COVENANTS 124 THROUGH 132

By the spring of 1839 the Saints were settling in Illinois at a bend of the Mississippi River. They named their new city Nauvoo, from a Hebrew word meaning "beautiful." Between 1841 and 1843 the Prophet received revelations that increased the Saints' understanding of temple blessings, including baptism for the dead, the endowment, and celestial marriage (D&C 124; 132). The Prophet's interest in the temple was evidenced in two letters he wrote on this subject (D&C 127; 128) while in hiding from his Missouri persecutors. Those two sections are not designated as revelations but contain the Prophet's inspired instructions on a wide variety of subjects.

DOCTRINE AND COVENANTS 121:41-46
What is the meaning of certain archaic words in these
beautiful and often-quoted instructions and promises?

Persuasion has taken on the sense of inducing a person to do something almost against his will, but in Doctrine and Covenants 121:41 the Lord specifies that our influence should be exerted only in the spirit of patience and love. *Betimes* in verse 43 means "in good season or time; before it is [too] late" (Webster, *American Dictionary*). In other words, we should respond promptly to the Spirit's direction. *Bowels* in verse 45 is understood to mean all the internal organs, including the heart, and represents "the seat of pity or kindness; hence, tenderness, compassion, a scriptural sense" (Webster, *American Dictionary*). The assurance of verse 45 that "the doctrine of the priesthood shall distill" upon us suggests that if we are worthy, we will be directed and feel comfortable as we act as God's representatives in blessing others. Similarly, the promise of verse 46 that our "dominion" will come "without compulsory means" suggests that our influence for good will be a natural result of our virtuous service.

DOCTRINE AND COVENANTS 124:23
What was the "corner-stone" visitors were to contemplate?

In this revelation, the Lord directed that two buildings be erected in Nauvoo: an inn to be known as "the Nauvoo House" (see D&C 124:22–24, 56–83), and the Nauvoo Temple (see vv. 25–44).

The "corner-stone" that guests in the Nauvoo House were to contemplate was identified in verse 2 as the stake that had been established at Nauvoo. In an earlier revelation the Lord had challenged the Saints in Zion and in her stakes to live so their "light may be a standard for the nations" (D&C 115:5). Hence, while enjoying accommodations in the Nauvoo House, visitors could observe at close range the Saints' example. Because it was thus a kind of missionary project, the Lord required that those who invested in the Nauvoo House should have a testimony of the restored gospel (see v. 119).

DOCTRINE AND COVENANTS 124:27–30
What functions do temples have other than being places where sacred ordinances are performed?

Not all latter-day temples have been designed primarily for ordinances. The Kirtland Temple, for example, served mostly other purposes. After decades of studying ancient Near Eastern religions, noted Latter-day Saint scholar Dr. Hugh Nibley concluded that these ancient peoples regarded temples as "meeting-places at which men at specific times attempted to make contact with the powers above" ("What Is a Temple?" 231).

Temples have served two main functions: as places of revelation or contact between heaven and earth, and as places for sacred priesthood ordinances. Elder James E. Talmage affirmed that a temple "is characterized not alone as the place where God reveals Himself to man, but also as the House wherein prescribed ordinances of the Priesthood are solemnized" (*House of the Lord*, 17).

The Kirtland Temple did not have a baptismal font or other facilities specifically designed for ordinances, and its dedicatory prayer spoke of only the first of the two purposes (see D&C 109:5). By the time the Nauvoo Temple was built, however, temple ordinances had been restored, so facilities for them were provided. Both purposes of temples are reflected in the Lord's instructions that the Nauvoo Temple should be a place where he might come to give revelations and that it should contain a font for vicarious baptisms (see D&C 124:27–30).

DOCTRINE AND COVENANTS 124:59
Were Joseph Smith's descendants to preside over the Church?

Doctrine and Covenants 124:59 considers the rights of those who invested in the construction of the Nauvoo House and has nothing to do with succession in the First Presidency. This verse simply affirms that Joseph Smith's heirs were to inherit his stock in the house according to the pattern commonly followed in the world. Note how similar inheritances were promised to others (see D&C 124:69, 74, 77).

Revelations provide the key to the correct pattern of succession. {See D&C 43:1–4; 107:22–26.}

DOCTRINE AND COVENANTS 124:124
In what sense do patriarchs hold the sealing keys?
What does it mean to be "sealed up unto the day of redemption"?

President Joseph Fielding Smith taught that patriarchs' sealing power is only conditional: "The patriarch has a right to seal a member up to come forth in the morning of the first resurrection, based upon his or her faithfulness, and that is all" (*Doctrines of Salvation*, 3:171). This promise is essentially encouragement to live worthy of receiving exaltation in the celestial kingdom.

DOCTRINE AND COVENANTS 124:133–40
What is the significance of "standing" and "traveling"?

As used in the revelations, the word *standing* seems to refer to functions within the Church while *traveling* denotes external responsibilities. For example, the Quorum of the Twelve is identified as a "traveling presiding high council" (D&C 107:33), whereas "standing high councils" function within stakes (v. 36). Similarly, high priests are called "standing presidents" (D&C 124:133–34), and elders are designated "standing ministers" (v. 137). On the other hand, the seventy, who are to be "especial witnesses unto the Gentiles and in all the world" (D&C 107:25), are designated "traveling ministers" (v. 97) or "traveling elders" (D&C 124:138–39).

DOCTRINE AND COVENANTS 128:3
What is the origin of the "ward" as a local Church unit?

At the time the words in this section of the Doctrine and Covenants were written, *ward* meant "a certain district, division or quarter of a town or city" (Webster, *American Dictionary*). Nauvoo was divided into wards, and it was here that for the first time bishops were assigned to preside over these units.

DOCTRINE AND COVENANTS 128:8–9
Can a clerk's failure to keep a written record deny us blessings we have earned?

A superficial reading of Doctrine and Covenants 128 may leave such an impression, but a closer look indicates otherwise. Verse 8 emphasizes the "power of the priesthood" and suggests that "whatsoever you record on earth shall be recorded in heaven" is just a variation of "whatsoever you bind on earth shall be bound in heaven."

According to verse 9, if an ordinance is to be binding, it must meet three requirements: (1) It must be done by proper authority and in the name of Jesus Christ; (2) it must be performed "truly and faithfully," or in other words, correctly; and (3) an accurate record must be kept.

As part of this last requirement, a "recorder or eye witness" must be present (v. 2). The Prophet Joseph Smith instructed: "It will be necessary, in the Grand Council, that these things be testified to by competent witnesses. Therefore let the recording and witnessing of baptisms for the dead be carefully attended to from this time forth" (*History of the Church*, 5:141). Assuming that these instructions are followed, the lack of a record suggests that the ordinance has not been performed—and it is the ordinance rather than the written record that binds in heaven.

President John Taylor suggested another possibility. Not all earthly records are kept with paper and ink. "Man himself is a self-registering machine, . . . all the various senses of the body are so many media whereby man lays up for himself a record which perhaps nobody else is acquainted with but himself; and when the time comes for that record to be unfolded all men that have eyes to see, and ears to hear, will be able to read all things as God Himself reads them and comprehends them" (in *Journal of Discourses*, 26:31).

DOCTRINE AND COVENANTS 128:18
Why is a "welding link" to our fathers necessary?
Why can't we be saved without them?

Paraphrasing the words of Paul (see Hebrews 11:40), Joseph Smith wrote that "the fathers" cannot be made perfect without us. They depend on us to perform necessary saving ordinances vicariously in their behalf. The Prophet also asserted that we cannot be made perfect without them. Those who are exalted in the highest degree of the celestial kingdom will be organized into a grand family structure with our Heavenly Father at the head. We need to be tied in with that great organization, and that is done along the lines of our family lineage. Hence we must establish a "welding link" from generation to generation, and that is done by means of sacred temple ordinances.

Elder Orson F. Whitney explained: "The Prophet says that there must be 'a welding link between the fathers and the children'—the fathers in heaven yearning over their children on earth; and therefore was Elijah sent. His keys empower the living to do saving work for the dead and seal them up to come forth in the first resurrection; 'to seal those who dwell on earth to those who dwell in heaven.' . . . The welding link is baptism for the dead, with other vicarious work now going on in the temples that God's people have erected. You brethren and sisters who labor in these temples may cherish in your souls the sweet conviction that you are helping to bind together the gospel dispensations and assisting to advance the mighty purposes of God" (in Conference Report, Oct. 1920, 35).

DOCTRINE AND COVENANTS 128:19
What is meant by the reference to "the dews of Carmel"?

Unusually heavy dew falls on the Carmel mountain range near the coast of northern Israel—a fact Joseph Smith likely did not know by any means other than revelation. Just as these dews distill on the ground, even so will the glad tidings of the gospel envelop and bless the faithful.

DOCTRINE AND COVENANTS 128:20–21
What more is known about the events referred to in these verses?

In Doctrine and Covenants 128:20–21 the Prophet exultantly reviews some of the great events of the Restoration. Additional information is provided about one of those events—the location where Peter, James, and John restored the Melchizedek Priesthood. "The chamber of old Father Whitmer" is the room in the Whitmers' log home where the Church was organized 6 April 1830; the revelation mentioned here is "unquestionably" the occasion in June of 1829 when the Lord instructed Joseph Smith concerning priesthood ordinations

(*History of the Church*, 1:60–61). "The voice of Gabriel" may refer to the appearance of Elias in the Kirtland Temple. {See D&C 110:12.} Nothing further is known concerning the identity or appearance of Raphael. These verses are the only record we have of the appearances of Michael or Adam.

DOCTRINE AND COVENANTS 129
Why will the various categories of messengers respond as described here?

Joseph Smith explained that there are two categories of messengers from heaven. One is angels, which are translated or resurrected beings with tangible bodies (see *History of the Church*, 4:425). These messengers are employed when priesthood authority is restored because this is done by the laying on of hands. Such beings of course would respond when invited to shake hands. The other is spirits, which may be either "unembodied" (still in their premortal existence) or "disembodied" (in the postmortal spirit world). Not having tangible bodies, they would not extend a hand we could not feel.

Only one category of messengers can come from Satan—spirits, because the resurrection of the unjust is yet future. {See D&C 76:17.} One might suppose that these devils would refrain from shaking hands to make us believe they come from God. But there is something, perhaps a divine law, that compels them to respond as verse 8 specifies. Or "perhaps he cannot help himself. He knows better, but he cannot pass up the opportunity to shock and deceive" (Preece, *Learning to Love the Doctrine and Covenants*, 375).

We may not need to use these keys to detect whether messengers come from God or from Satan. We are, however, almost constantly faced with discerning whether an idea or influence is of God or not. Fortunately we have the Holy Ghost to help us discern properly (see D&C 46:23; 50:15–22).

DOCTRINE AND COVENANTS 130:13
Where may this earlier revelation be found?

This "earlier revelation" is a reference to the prophecy on war (see D&C 87).

DOCTRINE AND COVENANTS 130:14–17
Isn't this a prediction that the Second Coming would occur in 1890?

Because the Second Coming did not occur in 1890, the year Joseph Smith would have turned eighty-five years of age, some critics have suggested that Doctrine and Covenants 130 is a false prophecy. Note, however, that verse 15 simply promises that Joseph Smith would "see the face of the Son of Man." Joseph himself wondered whether this "referred to the beginning of the millennium or to some previous appearing" (v. 16). An earlier revelation had made it clear that no one knows the exact time of the Lord's advent, "nor shall they know until he comes" (D&C 49:7). The Prophet correctly concluded that the Lord would not come before 1890 (see D&C 130:17).

DOCTRINE AND COVENANTS 131:2
What is the difference between "the new and everlasting covenant" and "the new and everlasting covenant of marriage"?

Because in Doctrine and Covenants 131 the Lord is discussing the exalted state that can be inherited only by those who have worthily entered celestial marriage, he particularly emphasizes the importance of this "new and everlasting covenant of marriage." That covenant should not be confused with the "new and everlasting covenant" that is the gospel as a whole. {See D&C 22.} While "baptism is the gate to the celestial kingdom," affirmed Elder Bruce R. McConkie, "celestial marriage is the gate to an exaltation in the highest heaven within the celestial world" (*Mormon Doctrine*, 118).

DOCTRINE AND COVENANTS 131:5
Why is it important to receive "the more sure word of prophecy" and how can we do so?

Receiving the assurance called "the more sure word of prophecy" (D&C 131:5) is essentially the same thing as being "sealed by the Holy Spirit of promise" (D&C 76:53) or making our "calling and election sure" (2 Peter 1:10). {See D&C 76:53.} Achieving this lofty spiritual goal prepares us to enjoy the further remarkable privilege of receiving the Second Comforter—meeting the Savior face to face. {See D&C 67:10.}

"The first great revelation that a person needs to get is *to know the divinity of the work*," explained Elder Bruce R. McConkie (*How to Get*

Personal Revelation, 8). Then, building on this testimony, we should constantly strive to keep the commandments and grow spiritually to the point we are worthy to inherit eternal life. The ultimate revelation that we should seek to obtain from the Holy Ghost is the assurance that our calling and election has been made sure. Elder McConkie challenged us to live so that we might "have the whisperings of the Spirit in [our] heart and soul and, in addition, can see visions, entertain angels, behold the face of the Lord" (*How to Get Personal Revelation,* 1).

The apostle Peter recalled the marvelous experience on the "holy mount" when he and his brethren beheld the transfigured Lord and heard the voice of God from heaven. Now he declared that he had an even "more sure word of prophecy" (2 Peter 1:18–19). He challenges us to give diligence to make our calling and election sure by adding "to your faith virtue; and to virtue knowledge; and to knowledge temperance; and to temperance patience; and to patience godliness; and to godliness brotherly kindness; and to brotherly kindness charity" (vv. 5–7).

Reflecting on Peter's words, the Prophet Joseph Smith expounded: "Though they might hear the voice of God and know that Jesus was the Son of God, this would be no evidence that their election and calling was made sure, that they had part with Christ, and were joint heirs with Him. They then would want that more sure word of prophecy, that they were sealed in the heavens and the promise of eternal life in the kingdom of God. Then, having this promise sealed unto them, it was an anchor to the soul, sure and steadfast." The Prophet then exhorted: "Go on and continue to call upon God until you make your calling and election sure for yourselves, by obtaining this more sure word of prophecy, and wait patiently for the promise until you obtain it" (*Teachings of the Prophet Joseph Smith,* 298–99).

After defining "the more sure word of prophecy," Joseph Smith taught that "it is impossible for a man to be saved in ignorance" of this saving witness (D&C 131:6). "If a man be ignorant of the terms on which salvation is predicated," reasoned Elder James E. Talmage, "he is unable to comply therewith, and consequently fails to attain what otherwise might have been his eternal gain" (*Vitality of Mormonism,* 268).

The great gift of eternal life "may not, of course, be fully realized during earth life," pointed out Elder Marion G. Romney. "An assurance that it will be obtained in the world to come may, however, be had in this world. As a matter of fact, the blessings of the celestial kingdom are promised only to those who have such an assurance." This blessing may not be realized in mortality, but we should be striving for it. Elder Romney concluded that it "is within the reach of us all, because it is not to be paid in money nor in any of this world's goods but in righteous living. What is required is wholehearted devotion to the gospel and unreserved allegiance to The Church of Jesus Christ of Latter-day Saints" (in Conference Report, Oct. 1949, 41, 43).

DOCTRINE AND COVENANTS 132:24
What is meant by "eternal lives"?

Beginning in verse 19 of Doctrine and Covenants 132, the Lord outlines the remarkable blessings to be enjoyed by those who are exalted in the celestial kingdom. In verse 24 he paraphrases the well-known statement in John 17:3. President Charles W. Penrose explained that "eternal lives" means "more than life, more than mere existence, it means perpetual increase of posterity, worlds without end" (in Conference Report, Oct. 1921, 22). President Harold B. Lee reasoned that "if marriage then was for the purpose of the organizing of spirits before the world was formed and for 'multiplying and replenishing the earth' on which we now live, surely there must likewise be a divine purpose in its being continued after the resurrection. This purpose is declared by the Lord to be for 'a continuation of the seeds forever and ever' [D&C 132:19]" (*Teachings of Harold B. Lee,* 238).

DOCTRINE AND COVENANTS 132:26
Does being married in the temple guarantee that we will be exalted?

"Verse 26, in Section 132, is the most abused passage in any scripture," asserted President Joseph Fielding Smith. "The Lord has never promised any soul that he may be taken into exaltation without the spirit of repentance. While repentance is not stated in this passage, yet it is, and must be implied" (*Doctrines of Salvation,* 2:95). Elder Harold B. Lee concurred: "Among us there are folks who are interpreting the twenty-sixth verse of the 132nd section of the Doctrine and Covenants to mean that if by some hook or crook we can get into the temple and be married, we are sure of an exaltation regardless of what we may do thereafter. . . . The Lord means that we can be forgiven of all kinds of sin except the unpardonable sin, *if we truly repent,* and shall be forgiven" (*Teachings of Harold B. Lee,* 111; emphasis in original).

"Those who have been married in the temples for eternity,"

pointed out Elder Bruce R. McConkie, "know that the ceremony itself expressly conditions the receipt of all promised blessings upon the subsequent faithfulness of the husband and wife. Making one's calling and election sure is in addition to celestial marriage and results from undeviating and perfect devotion to the cause of righteousness. Those married in the temple can never under any circumstances gain exaltation unless they keep the commandments of God and abide in the covenant of marriage which they have taken upon themselves" (*Mormon Doctrine*, 118).

Doctrine and Covenants 132:26 itself imposes some important restrictions. Not only must a couple be married in the temple by proper authority but they must also be "sealed by the Holy Spirit of promise." This means that they must have reached the point that they were judged worthy to receive the eternal blessings promised by this sacred ordinance. {See D&C 76:53.} In other words they must have made their calling and election sure. {See D&C 131:5.} Obviously this blessing requires a degree of faithfulness far beyond even the high requirements to receive a temple recommend.

Those who are to be exalted cannot "shed innocent blood." In verse 27 the Lord defines that those who commit this offense in effect "assent unto my death, after ye have received my new and everlasting covenant." They "crucified him unto themselves and put him to an open shame" (D&C 76:35).

Those who have committed sins must thoroughly repent. Part of the process may need to involve their being "destroyed in the flesh" and being "delivered unto the buffetings of Satan" (D&C 132:26). The exact nature of these sufferings may not be known, but concerning their extent the Lord declared: "How sore you know not, how exquisite you know not, yea, how hard to bear you know not" (D&C 19:15). Even though the reward of exaltation would make such terrible suffering worthwhile, it is far better to avoid it by keeping the commandments and receiving the peace that is promised by so doing (see D&C 59:23).

DOCTRINE AND COVENANTS 132:38
Did God really authorize men to have concubines?

We may think of a concubine as a mistress with whom a man has illicit relations, but a dictionary published at the time Doctrine and Covenants 132 was written defined *concubine* as "a wife of inferior condition. . . . Such were Hagar and Keturah, the concubines of Abraham" (Webster, *American Dictionary*). The Lord affirms that he permitted David and Solomon to have wives and concubines and that they sinned only when they took what he had not authorized. Solomon had seven hundred wives and three hundred concubines! The vast majority of them undoubtedly were not given by the Lord, because they turned Solomon's heart from God (see 1 Kings 11:3–4). The Book of Mormon prophet Jacob denounced those who used Solomon's grossly unworthy example to excuse their own whoredoms (see Jacob 2:23–24).

DOCTRINE AND COVENANTS 132:51
What was Emma's test?

"No indication is given here or elsewhere about what the Lord had commanded the Prophet Joseph to offer to his wife, but the context seems to suggest that it was a special test of faith similar to the great test of Abraham's faith when the Lord commanded him to sacrifice Isaac. Beyond that, it is useless to speculate, for the record is silent" (*Doctrine and Covenants Student Manual*, 334).

SOME FURTHER REVELATIONS

DOCTRINE AND COVENANTS 133 THROUGH 138

AND OFFICIAL DECLARATIONS 1 AND 2

The revelations recorded in the ending sections of the Doctrine and Covenants were received between 1831 and 1978. Section 133 is called the "Appendix," and section 134 is a declaration of beliefs about laws and governments. In section 135 we find an inspired appraisal of Joseph Smith's contributions. Section 136, the only revelation given through Brigham Young that has been included in the Doctrine Covenants, contains important practical instructions to the pioneers. Sections 137 and 138 were added to the canon of Latter-day Saint scripture in 1976. The two Official Declarations announce revelations ending the practice of plural marriage and extending priesthood blessings to worthy males of all races. These sacred communications provide an important foundation for the activities of the Church as it expands worldwide.

DOCTRINE AND COVENANTS 133
Why is this revelation out of chronological order?

Being regarded as an appendix, Doctrine and Covenants 133 stands at the end of the revelations received through Joseph Smith. Like the "preface" (D&C 1), section 133 was received at the November 1831 conference that initially approved publishing the revelations in book form. Though given at the same time (between sections 66 and 68), these two revelations now stand at opposite ends of the Doctrine and Covenants. Both treat the same general theme—preparing for the latter days.

DOCTRINE AND COVENANTS 133:4–14
Does the "gathering" always require moving from one place to another?

At first the Lord asked the Saints to congregate in one place but explained that the time would come when many other gathering places would be established. {See D&C 29:7–8.} In section 133 the Lord introduced the further concept of a spiritual gathering: "Go ye out from Babylon. Be ye clean. . . . Go ye out . . . from the midst of wickedness, which is spiritual Babylon" (vv. 5, 14). Thus wherever they lived, the Saints could stay in their homes while gathering out of the world into the Lord's Church.

DOCTRINE AND COVENANTS 133:23–24
What evidence is there that the earth's continents and islands once were a single land mass?

In the mid twentieth century individuals increasingly pointed out how the earth's continents appear to be like giant pieces of a puzzle and might once have been parts of a single land mass. This "continental drift" theory was not generally considered seriously by most scientists. In more recent decades, however, studies of strata and magnetic patterns in rocks on opposite sides of oceans suggest that they once were together. Today "plate tectonics" is the name given to the concept that the earth's surface is made up of huge plates that are constantly moving against one another.

DOCTRINE AND COVENANTS 134:9
Shouldn't our politics be influenced by the gospel?

Latter-day Saints believe in a separation of church and state in the sense that neither of these institutions should dominate the other. Still, there is not a total separation, because we as Church members are commanded to seek and uphold wise and good men (see D&C 98:10) and because religious groups may appeal to the state for protection. Doctrine and Covenants 134:9 concurs with provisions of the United States Constitution that one religion should not be supported by government while others are prohibited and that freedom of religion must not be infringed.

The gospel may be thought of as our complete way of life. Hence, it should influence our views on politics as well as on all other subjects. Church leaders have the responsibility to counsel the Saints on moral issues that affect our ability to live the gospel. Still, we are instructed to become involved in civic and political affairs as citizens rather than as representatives of the Church.

DOCTRINE AND COVENANTS 135:3
What did Joseph Smith do "for the salvation of men in this world"?

President Joseph F. Smith, the prophet's nephew, summed up some of his accomplishments: "He opened up communication with the heavens in his youth. He brought forth the Book of Mormon, which contains the fullness of the Gospel; and the revelations contained in the Book of Doctrine and Covenants; restored the holy Priesthood unto man; established and organized The Church of Jesus Christ of Latter-day Saints." He established settlements of the Saints in New York, Ohio, Missouri and Illinois and directed the construction of temples at Kirtland and Nauvoo. Obviously the fulness of the gospel as restored through Joseph Smith together with the Church and its authoritative ordinances are essential to our salvation. As President Joseph F. Smith asked, "Where shall we go to find another man that has accomplished the one thousandth part of good that Joseph Smith accomplished?" (in *Journal of Discourses*, 24:14–15).

DOCTRINE AND COVENANTS 137–38
What is significant about the time when these two revelations were added to the standard works?

The revelations in Doctrine and Covenants 137 and 138 were added to the standard works in 1976. They were placed in the Pearl of Great Price temporarily but became part of the new edition of the Doctrine and Covenants published in 1981.

Both sections provide scriptural support for the important doctrine of salvation of the dead. Section 137 includes the declaration that "all who have died without a knowledge of this gospel, who would have received it if they had been permitted to tarry, shall be heirs of the celestial kingdom of God" (v. 7). Section 138 sheds light on how the Savior launched the preaching of the gospel in the spirit world.

In 1976 there were only sixteen Latter-day Saint temples in service. Within the next ten years that total increased to forty-five. Developments in computer technology dramatically aided genealogical research. Hence these two revelations being placed in the standard works gave valuable impetus to this great expansion in temple service.

OFFICIAL DECLARATIONS 1 AND 2
Why are these two items not given numbers as previous sections were?

Both Official Declarations are inspired announcements that significant revelations had been received. For example, Official Declaration 1 is not the revelation that ended plural marriages. A careful reading indicates that this practice had already been suspended. President Wilford Woodruff subsequently described the earlier revelation that had brought the change. His accounts were added to the Doctrine and Covenants in the 1981 edition and are found on pages 291 through 293.

Similarly, the revelation extending priesthood blessings to men of all races was received during a remarkable experience in the Salt Lake Temple on 1 June 1978. For more than two hours the First Presidency and the Twelve considered this matter. "There was a marvelous outpouring of unity, oneness, and agreement in the council." President Spencer W. Kimball then led the group in prayer on this matter. "It was during this prayer that the revelation came," Elder Bruce R. McConkie recalled. "The Spirit of the Lord rested mightily upon us all; we felt something akin to what happened on the day of Pentecost and at the dedication of the Kirtland Temple" (in *Priesthood*, 128). The announcement known as Official Declaration 2 was released one week later.

SOURCES CITED

Anderson, A. Gary. "Thomas B. Marsh: The Preparation and Conversion of the Emerging Apostle," in *Regional Studies in Latter-day Saint Church History, New York.* Provo, Utah: Brigham Young University, Department of Church History and Doctrine, 1992.

Backman, Milton V., Jr., and Richard O. Cowan. *Joseph Smith and the Doctrine and Covenants.* Salt Lake City: Deseret Book, 1992.

Ballard, Melvin J. *Three Degrees of Glory.* Salt Lake City: Magazine Printing, 1922.

Benson, Ezra Taft. *The Teachings of Ezra Taft Benson.* Salt Lake City: Bookcraft, 1988.

Berger, Kathleen Stassen, and Ross A. Thompson. *The Developing Person through Childhood and Adolescence.* 3d ed. New York: Worth Publishers, 1991.

Cannon, Donald Q., and Lyndon W. Cook. *Far West Record: Minutes of The Church of Jesus Christ of Latter-day Saints, 1830–1844.* Salt Lake City: Deseret Book, 1983.

Church News. A weekly supplement of the Deseret News. Salt Lake City, 1931–.

Church History in the Fulness of Times [manual for Religion 341–343]. Salt Lake City: The Church of Jesus Christ of Latter-day Saints, 1989.

The Church Welfare Plan. Salt Lake City: Deseret Sunday School Union, 1946.

Clark, James R., comp. *Messages of the First Presidency of The Church of Jesus Christ of Latter-day Saints.* 6 vols. Salt Lake City: Bookcraft, 1965–75.

Collected Discourses, Delivered by President Wilford Woodruff, His Two Counselors, the Twelve Apostles, and Others. Comp. Brian H. Stuy. 5 vols. Burbank, Calif.: B.H.S. Publishing, 1987–92.

Compton's Encyclopedia and Fact-Index. Chicago: Compton's Learning, 1994.

Conference Report. Salt Lake City: Church of Jesus Christ of Latter-day Saints, 1897–.

Conference Report of the Denmark, Finland, Norway, and Sweden Area Conference held in Stockholm, Sweden Aug. 16, 17, and 18, 1974. Salt Lake City: The Church of Jesus Christ of Latter-day Saints, 1975.

Conference Report of Korea Area Conference held in Seoul, Korea Aug. 15, 16, and 17, 1975. Salt Lake City: The Church of Jesus Christ of Latter-day Saints, 1977.

Conference Report of Mexico and Central America Area General Conference held in Mexico City, Mexico Aug. 25, 26, and 27, 1972. Salt Lake City: The Church of Jesus Christ of Latter-day Saints, 1973.

Deseret Weekly. Salt Lake City: Deseret News, 1888–98.

Doctrine and Covenants Student Manual [for Religion 324–325]. Salt Lake City: The Church of Jesus Christ of Latter-day Saints, 1981.

155

SOURCES CITED

SOURCES CITED

Doxey, Roy W. *The Latter-day Prophets and the Doctrine and Covenants.* 4 vols. Salt Lake City: Deseret Book, 1964.

Draper, Richard D. "Light, Truth, and Grace: Three Interrelated Salvation Themes in Doctrine and Covenants 93," in *Doctrines for Exaltation: The 1989 Sperry Symposium on the Doctrine and Covenants.* Salt Lake City: Deseret Book, 1989.

Elders' Journal. Chattanooga: Southern States Mission, 1906.

Ensign. Salt Lake City: The Church of Jesus Christ of Latter-day Saints, 1971–.

Hinckley, Bryant S. *Sermons and Missionary Services of Melvin Joseph Ballard.* Salt Lake City: Deseret Book, 1949.

Hymns of The Church of Jesus Christ of Latter-day Saints. Salt Lake City: The Church of Jesus Christ of Latter-day Saints, 1985.

Improvement Era. Salt Lake City: Young Men's and Young Women's Mutual Improvement Associations, 1897–1970.

Jackson, Kent. P. "Revelations Concerning Isaiah." In *The Doctrine and Covenants.* Ed. Kent P. Jackson and Robert L. Millet. Studies in Scripture Series, vol. 1. Sandy, Utah: Randall Book, 1984.

Journal of Discourses. 26 vols. London: Latter-day Saints' Book Depot, 1854–86.

Kimball, Spencer W. *Faith Precedes the Miracle.* Salt Lake City: Deseret Book, 1972.

———. *The Miracle of Forgiveness.* Salt Lake City: Bookcraft, 1969.

———. *That You May Not Be Deceived.* Brigham Young University Speeches of the Year. Provo, 11 Nov. 1959.

Lee, Harold B. *The Teachings of Harold B. Lee.* Comp. Clyde J. Williams. Salt Lake City: Bookcraft, 1996.

———. "Be Loyal to the Royal within You," in *Speeches of the Year, 1973.* Provo: Brigham Young University Press, 1974.

Ludlow, Daniel H., ed. *Encyclopedia of Mormonism.* 5 vols. New York: Macmillan, 1992.

Madsen, Truman G. *Joseph Smith the Prophet.* Salt Lake City: Bookcraft, 1989.

Matthews, Robert J. *"A Plainer Translation": Joseph Smith's Translation of the Bible, a History and Commentary.* Provo, Utah: Brigham Young University Press, 1985.

McConkie, Bruce R. *Doctrinal New Testament Commentary.* 3 vols. Salt Lake City: Bookcraft, 1973.

———. *The Millennial Messiah: The Second Coming of the Son of Man.* Salt Lake City: Deseret Book, 1982.

———. *Mormon Doctrine.* 2d ed. Salt Lake City: Bookcraft, 1966.

———. *The Mortal Messiah: From Bethlehem to Calvary.* 4 vols. Salt Lake City: Deseret Book, 1980–81.

———. *The Promised Messiah.* Salt Lake City: Deseret Book, 1978.

———. *How to Get Personal Revelation.* Brigham Young University Speeches of the Year. Provo, 11 Oct. 1966.

Millennial Star. Liverpool, England, 1840–1970.

156

Millet, Robert L., and Larry E. Dahl. *The Capstone of Our Religion*. Salt Lake City: Bookcraft, 1989.

New Era. Salt Lake City: Church of Jesus Christ of Latter-day Saints, 1971–.

New International Version *Study Bible*. Kenneth Barker, ed. Grand Rapids, Mich.: Zondervan Bible Publishers, 1985.

New Jerusalem Bible. New York: Doubleday, 1990.

Nibley, Hugh W. "What Is a Temple? The Idea of the Temple in History," *Millennial Star*, Aug. 1958, 8.

Oaks, Dallin H. *The Lord's Way*. Salt Lake City: Deseret Book, 1991.

Otten, L. G., and C. M. Caldwell. *Sacred Truths of the Doctrine and Covenants*. 2 vols. 3d ed. Springville, Utah: LEMB, 1982.

Petersen, Mark E. *A Commitment to Temple Marriage*. Brigham Young University Speeches of the Year. Provo, 31 Oct. 1962.

Porter, Larry C., Milton V. Backman Jr., and Susan Easton Black. *Regional Studies in Latter-day Saint Church History: New York*. Provo, Utah: Brigham Young University, Department of Church History and Doctrine, 1992.

Porter, Larry C. "The Restoration of the Priesthood," *Religious Studies Center Newsletter*, May 1995.

Pratt, Parley Parker. *Autobiography of Parley Parker Pratt*. Ed. Parley P. Pratt Jr. 6th ed. Salt Lake City: Deseret Book, 1966.

Preece, Michael J. *Learning to Love the Doctrine and Covenants*. Salt Lake City: MJP Publishing, 1988.

Priesthood. Salt Lake City: Deseret Book, 1981.

Roberts, B. H. *A Comprehensive History of The Church of Jesus Christ of Latter-day Saints*. 6 vols. Provo, Utah: Brigham Young University Press, 1965.

———. *Defense of the Faith and the Saints*. 2 vols. Salt Lake City: Deseret News, 1907.

Romney, Marion G. *The Blessings of an Honest Tithe*. Brigham Young University Speeches of the Year. Provo, 5 Nov. 1960.

Smith, Hyrum M., and Janne M. Sjodahl. *The Doctrine and Covenants Commentary*. Salt Lake City: Deseret Book, 1951.

Smith, Joseph. *History of the Church of Jesus Christ of Latter-day Saints*. Ed. B. H. Roberts. 2d ed. rev. 7 vols. Salt Lake City: Deseret Book, 1948.

———. *Teachings of the Prophet Joseph Smith*. Sel. Joseph Fielding Smith. Salt Lake City: Deseret News Press, 1938.

Smith, Joseph F. *Gospel Doctrine*. Salt Lake City: Deseret Book, 1919.

Smith, Joseph Fielding. *Answers to Gospel Questions*. 5 vols. Salt Lake City: Deseret Book, 1957–66.

———. *Church History and Modern Revelation*. 2 vols. Salt Lake City: Council of the Twelve Apostles of The Church of Jesus Christ of Latter-day Saints, 1953.

———. *Doctrines of Salvation*. Comp. Bruce R. McConkie. 3 vols. Salt Lake City: Bookcraft, 1954–56.

———. *The Restoration of All Things*. Salt Lake City: Deseret News Press, 1945.

———. *The Way to Perfection*. Salt Lake City: Deseret News Press, 1931.

Sperry, Sidney B. *Doctrine and Covenants Compendium*. Salt Lake City: Bookcraft, 1960.

Talmage, James E. *Articles of Faith*. Salt Lake City: The Church of Jesus Christ of Latter-day Saints, 1966.

———. *House of the Lord*. Salt Lake City: Bookcraft, 1962.

———. *Jesus the Christ*. Salt Lake City: Deseret Book, 1951.

———. *The Vitality of Mormonism*. Salt Lake City: Deseret News Press, 1919.

Times and Seasons. Nauvoo, Illinois: Taylor and Woodruff, 1839–46. Reprint. 6 vols. Independence, Mo.: Independence Press, 1986.

Webster, Noah. *American Dictionary of the English Language*. 1828. Reprint, San Francisco: Foundation for American Christian Education, 1980.

Widtsoe, John A. *Evidences and Reconciliations*. Ed. G. Homer Durham. 3 vols. in 1. Salt Lake City: Bookcraft, 1960.

———. *Joseph Smith—Seeker After Truth—Prophet of God*. Salt Lake City: Deseret News Press, 1939.

———. *The Message of the Doctrine and Covenants*. Ed. G. Homer Durham. Salt Lake City: Bookcraft, 1969.

———. *Priesthood and Church Government*. Salt Lake City: Deseret Book, 1954.

———. *Program of The Church of Jesus Christ of Latter-day Saints*. 4th ed. Salt Lake City: Deseret Book, 1941.

Widtsoe, John A., and Leah D. Widtsoe. *The Word of Wisdom: A Modern Interpretation*. 2d ed. Salt Lake City: Deseret Book, 1937.

Woodbury, Lael. "The Origin and Uses of the Sacred Hosanna Shout" in *Sperry Lecture Series*. Provo, Utah: Brigham Young University Press, 1975.

Woodford, Robert J. "The Historical Development of the Doctrine and Covenants." Ph.D. dissertation, Brigham Young University, 1974.

Woodruff, Wilford. *The Discourses of Wilford Woodruff*. Comp. G. Homer Durham. Salt Lake City: Bookcraft, 1969.

Young, Brigham. *Discourses of Brigham Young*. Comp. John A. Widtsoe. Salt Lake City: Deseret Book, 1954 .

Young, Joseph, Sr. *History of the Organization of the Seventies*. Salt Lake City: Deseret News, 1878.

INDEX

and discernment, 144. *See also* Holy
  Spirit *and* Spirit
Holy Land, 62
Holy Spirit: denying the, 52–53; of
  promise, 88, 104–5, 148. *See also*
  Holy Ghost *and* Spirit
Home: breakdown of, 7; role of, 66
Hosanna Shout, 127–28
Hot drinks, 111–12
Hubble, 59
Hunter, Howard W., 77; on tithing, 135;
  on interest, 136
Hymns, 38–39

Immorality, 27; sexual, 54
Independence, congregation in, 42
Inspiration, 15
Intellect, 52
Intelligence, 105; and the glory of God,
  115–16
Israel, gathering of, 128

Jackson, Kent, 132
Jehovah, 49–50. *See also* Jesus Christ
Jerusalem, New, 96
Jesse, root and rod of, 131–32
Jesus Christ: second coming of, 3, 5,
  43–44, 95; suffering of, 22; date of
  birth of, 23–24; taking name of, 26;
  gospel of, 32–33; as spokesman, 45;
  and God, 49–50; signs of coming of,
  62; witness of, 80; blaspheming, 87;
  acknowledging, 91; Spirit of,
  99–100; at Adam-ondi-Ahman, 134
Jews: Lamanites as remnant of, 23;
  receive gospel, 61; and nation of
  Israel, 128
John the Apostle, 114
John the Baptist, 19–20, 40, 114; as
  forerunner, 128
Joseph Smith Translation, 48–49, 57–58
Journal, keeping a, 64–65
Joy, fulness of, 16
Judah, blood of, 22
Judas, 44
Judgment: depending on own, 2, 76;
  factors in, 96
Justification, 25

Keys, 112; priesthood, 129
Kimball, Heber C., 63
Kimball, Spencer W.: on revelation, 41;
  on building up the Church, 43; on
  consecration, 56; on death, 57; on
  keeping a journal, 64–65; on
  Sabbath activity, 71; on revelation
  giving priesthood to all men, 153
Kingdom of God, 77
Kingdom of heaven, mysteries of the,
  123
Kingdoms, 85
King James Bible, 48–49
Kirtland: congregation in, 42;
  stronghold in, 76; Temple, 109,
  116–17, 127, 140; appearance of
  Elias in, Temple, 144
Kitchell, Ashbel, 65
Knight, Joseph, Sr., 34
Knowledge, 6, 52, 105, 115–16

Lamanites: as remnant of Jews, 23;
  mission to, 41–42, 51
"Last of all," 85
Latter-day Saints, 133
Laughter, excess of, 109–10
Law: celestial, 105; obeying
  constitutional, 118
Lee, Harold B.: on general conferences,
  4, 67; on Malachi's prophecy, 7; on
  role of women, 37; on call of
  president, 60; on pure hearts, 61–62;
  on correlation, 101; on education,
  107–8; on Quorum of Twelve, 123;
  on marriage, 147
Levi, sons of, 19
Licenses, 28
Light and truth, 116
Logic, 52
Lord, 65–66; relationship with, 100; of
  Sabaoth, 117. *See also* Jesus Christ
Lucifer, 86, 134
Lund, Anthon H., 71

Madsen, Truman G., 63
Malachi, prophecy of, 5
Man: role of, 37; creation of, 94
Marriage: eternal, 24–25, 32–33;
  celestial, 36; place of, 66; interfaith,